Mediumship for Beginners

An Essential Guide to Psychic Development, Clairvoyance, Scrying, and Channeling in Shamanism, Spiritualism, and Voodoo

Your Free Gift
(only available for a limited time)

Thanks for getting this book! If you want to learn more about various spirituality topics, then join Mari Silva's community and get a free guided meditation MP3 for awakening your third eye. This guided meditation mp3 is designed to open and strengthen ones third eye so you can experience a higher state of consciousness. Simply visit the link below the image to get started.

https://spiritualityspot.com/meditation

Table of Contents

Introduction

Do you want to develop your mediumship skills? Are you curious about the spirit world and how you can communicate with spirits? If so, this guide will teach you everything you need to know about communicating with the spirit world.

Developing your mediumship skills can be a rewarding and life-changing experience. It can also be a bit daunting, especially if you're just starting. This guide will ease you into the world of mediumship and provide you with all the information and resources you need to get started. You first need to understand that everyone can communicate with spirits. We were all born with this ability, but it is dormant for many of us. The good news is that it can be awakened. There are many different ways to develop your mediumship skills. While some people can effortlessly communicate with spirits, others must work harder to develop this innate skill.

One of the best ways to develop your mediumship skills is to find a mentor. A mentor is someone who has already developed their mediumship skills and who can help guide you on your journey. A good mentor will be able to teach you how to ground and protect yourself, how to recognize energy, and how to develop your clairs. Another great way to develop your mediumship skills is to study. There are many books and resources available on the topic of mediumship. Reading about different techniques and methods will help you develop your skills further. Many online courses can teach you about mediumship.

In "Mediumship for Beginners," you'll learn about the different types of mediumship, how to develop your mediumship skills, and how to communicate with spirits. The first section of this guide will introduce you to the basics of mediumship, including what it is and how it works. We'll also discuss different ways to develop your mediumship skills. In the second section, we'll explore the spirit world and teach you how to communicate with spirits. You'll also discover how to protect yourself from negative energy and how to cleanse and protect your space. Finally, we'll cover advanced topics, such as scrying and channeling.

To help you get started on your journey, we have included chapters covering the basics of mediumship, including how to recognize energy, develop your clairs, and scry. We have also included a chapter on advanced spirit communication methods. We hope you enjoy this guide and that it helps you to develop your mediumship skills. Whether you're just beginning your journey as a medium or looking to brush up on your skills, this informative guide will provide you with everything you need to know about communicating with the spirit world. So, let's get started!

Chapter 1: The Way of the Medium

Have you ever wondered whether or not communicating with the dead was possible? If so, you're not alone. Throughout history, man has attempted to contact the spirit world in various ways. This practice is known as mediumship. This can be defined as the ability to communicate with the dead or spirits. Mediums have this ability, and they use it to relay messages from the spirit world to the living.

Mediumship is the ability to communicate with spirits.
https://www.pexels.com/photo/assorted-tarot-cards-on-table-3088369/

Mediumship has been around since the dawn of time and has taken many different forms. In the early days, mediumship was often associated with shamanism and witchcraft. As time went on, however, it began to take on a more spiritualistic approach. This chapter will explore the history of mediumship and the different types that exist today. It will also introduce you to some genuine mediums working in the modern world.

What Is Mediumship?

Mediumship is the ability to communicate with spirits. This can be done in several ways, including through auditory or visual means. All people are born with the natural ability to connect with the dead, while some may need to develop their skills through practice and study. Mediums often use their abilities to provide comfort and closure to those who have lost loved ones. They may also be able to offer insights into the future or guidance on important life decisions. While some people are skeptical of mediumship, many believe it is a real and valuable gift.

By definition, a medium acts as an intermediary between the living and the dead. Mediums can bridge the gap between our world and the spirit world. They use their abilities to communicate with spirits and relay messages to the living. Mediums may also be able to see into the future or offer guidance on important life decisions. With their help, we can connect with our loved ones who have passed on and receive closure or comfort.

Abilities of a Medium

Communicating with the dead has been practiced since ancient times. To become a medium, you must first learn about the different abilities required for the job. One of the most essential abilities is that of clairvoyance or clear seeing. This allows the medium to see beyond the physical world and into the spirit realm. Another ability is clairaudience or clear hearing. This allows the medium to hear messages from the other side that are not normally audible to the human ear. In addition, mediums often have a strong sense of empathy, which allows them to feel the emotions of those who have passed on. By honing these skills, anyone can become a medium and help to connect with those who have died.

Mediumship Now and Then

In the past, mediums often worked as part of a spiritualist church, holding séances and conducting readings for the public. However, the use of mediumship began to decline in the early 20th century as people became more skeptical of the practice. In recent years, however, mediumship is more often seen as a personal practice. Many people use mediumship to connect with loved ones who have passed away, and some even use it to communicate with animals or other beings. As our world becomes more open to different spiritual belief systems, mediumship will likely continue to grow in popularity. Who knows what kind of amazing connections we'll make in the future?

Early History

Mediumship is a topic that has fascinated people for centuries. The early history of mediumship is shrouded in mystery, but there are some interesting theories about its origins. One theory suggests that mediumship developed as a way to contact the spirit world and gain guidance and wisdom from beyond. Others believe it is a natural human ability that various cultures have harnessed throughout history. Regardless of its origins, mediumship has played an essential role in many cultures and continues to do so today. Thanks to modern communication technology, anyone can now experience its wonders by connecting with a trusted psychic medium.

Spiritualism

During the 19th century, spiritualism became popular throughout the United States and Europe. At its core, spiritualism believes in the ability to communicate with the dead, and many people turned to mediums to receive messages from loved ones who had passed away. In addition to providing comfort and closure for grieving individuals, spiritualism also played a significant role in the development of mediumship.

Through their work with spirits, mediums began to develop heightened psychic abilities, which they then used to help others connect with the other side. As mediumship became more widely accepted, it became a legitimate form of communication, paving the way for future psychic research. Today, spiritualism is still practiced by millions of people worldwide, and its impact on religion and psychic research can still be felt.

Shamanism

Shamanism is a type of spiritual practice based on the belief that everything in the universe is connected. Shamans are spiritual guides who heal individuals and communities by connecting with the spirit world. To do this, they must first enter into a trance-like state, which allows them to travel to different planes of existence. Once they have made contact with the spirits, they can relay messages and advice that can help heal those in need.

Shamanism is an ancient practice that has been used by indigenous cultures all over the world. It is only in recent years, however, that shamanism has begun to enter the mainstream. As more people become interested in alternative forms of healing, shamanism is likely to continue to grow in popularity. If you're looking for a deeper connection to the spiritual world, shamanism may be the path for you.

Voodoo

Voodoo is a religion that originated in Haiti, but it has since spread to other parts of the world, including the United States. It is based on the belief that there is a spirit world that can interact with our own. Voodoo practitioners work with these spirits, or *loas*, to bring about positive change in their lives. They may also turn to the spirits for guidance and protection.

Voodoo is often associated with dark and black magic, but this is unrealistic. It is a religion that should be respected, just like any other. If you are interested in learning more, there are many resources available. Just remember to approach it with an open mind and a respectful attitude. Voodoo has always been a controversial topic. Some say it is the dark side of mediumship, while others claim it is simply another way to connect with the spirit world.

Modern Times

Nowadays, anyone can experience the wonder of mediumship by connecting with a trusted psychic medium. There are many different ways to do this, including online chat rooms, phone readings, and in-person sessions. No matter how you choose to connect, you can be sure that you'll receive accurate and helpful information from your medium.

If you are interested in connecting with a loved one who has passed away or simply want to get in touch with your spirituality, mediumship is a great way to do it. With the help of a psychic medium, you can explore the depths of your soul and discover answers to the questions that have been weighing heavily on your mind.

The Different Types of Mediumship

There are different types of mediumship, each with its unique skill set. Some mediums can see and speak to ghosts, while others can only communicate with them through psychometry, which is the ability to read objects touched by the deceased. Other mediums can channel the dead, allowing the ghosts to possess their bodies to speak through them. Finally, some mediums can astral project, leaving their bodies and traveling to the spirit world. Each type of mediumship has its strengths and weaknesses, and it is up to each medium to decide which type of communication is best for them.

1. Physical Mediumship

Physical mediumship is one of the most fascinating and controversial forms of mediumship. Physical mediums can materialize "spiritual beings" and produce other physical phenomena, such as levitation and teleportation. This type of activity is often associated with séances and Spiritualism, and it has been the subject of intense scientific scrutiny. Some physical mediums have been exposed as frauds, while others have been scientifically validated. Whether you believe in the paranormal or not, physical mediumship remains one of the most intriguing phenomena in the world.

2. Mental Mediumship

Mental mediumship is a psychic ability in which the medium telepathically receives information from the spirit world. In other words, the medium does not use any physical senses to receive communication from the spirits. Instead, the information is passed on through thoughts and feelings. Mental mediumship is a relatively rare ability, but it can be beneficial for spirit communication.

One of the benefits of mental mediumship is that it allows the spirit to communicate directly with the medium without having to use an intermediary. This can provide a more direct and personal form of communication than other methods, such as using a Ouija board or talking to a psychic. Additionally, mental mediumship is not limited by distance like some other forms of communication. The medium can receive information from anywhere worldwide, regardless of how far away they are. Mental mediumship is a powerful tool for anyone interested in communicating with the spirit world.

3. Spiritualist Mediumship

Spiritualist mediums are exceptionally skilled at connecting with the spirits of those who have passed away. This ability allows them to provide comfort and closure to the bereaved by delivering messages from loved ones who have crossed over. Mediumship can also be used to communicate with ancestors or other guides who can offer wisdom and guidance. While some people may be skeptical, a growing body of evidence suggests it is a real and powerful phenomenon.

4. Trance Mediumship

Trance mediumship is a type of mediumship in which the medium enters into a trance state to commune with the spirit world. The trance state is characterized by an altered state of consciousness, during which the medium becomes unaware of his surroundings and is instead completely focused on spirit communication.

While in a trance, the medium may exhibit strange behaviors, such as speaking in tongues or experiencing convulsions. However, these behaviors are not considered to be under the medium's control. Instead, they are seen as a manifestation of the spirit's presence. Trance mediumship is considered one of the most potent and authentic forms, as it allows for a direct connection to the spirit world.

5. Channeling

Channeling is one of the most well-known methods of mediumship, and it involves receiving messages from spirit guides or other nonphysical beings. The channeler goes into a trance-like state, and the entity speaks through them, using its vocal cords to communicate. Many people who channel say they feel like they are channeling energy rather than actual words, and the experience can be both powerful and transformative. Channeling can be used for guidance, healing, or simply to receive messages from loved ones who have passed on. While becoming a channeler is not always easy, anyone can learn how to do it with practice and patience.

6. Automatic Writing

Automatic writing is a type of channeling in which the medium goes into a trance-like state and allows spirits to dictate messages through their hand. This can be done with a pen and paper or even using a keyboard.

Many people who practice automatic writing claim that they can receive clear and concise messages from the other side, which can comfort those grieving. Automatic writing can also be used for divination purposes, as the messages received can offer insight into future events.

While anyone can try their hand at automatic writing, it is said that those who are naturally gifted at channeling are more likely to have success. Suppose you're interested in giving it a try. In that case, the best way to start is by sitting down in a quiet place with a pen and paper (or your laptop) and simply letting your hand move across the page or fingers across the keyboard. It may take some practice to get into the flow, but eventually, you should be able to receive messages from your deceased loved ones.

7. Direct Voice

One type of mediumship is called the direct voice. A direct voice medium channels a deceased loved one's voice – either in person or over the phone. The most famous example of a direct voice medium is Doris Stokes, who spoke to the dead through her television show in the 1970s and 1980s. People would call in, and she would relay messages from their deceased relatives.

Sometimes, the voices would speak through her directly, and at other times they would speak through a disembodied spirit she would see in the room. Direct voice mediumship is considered one of the most accurate forms of mediumship because it eliminates any possibility of fraud. If a medium is genuinely channeling a deceased loved one's voice, there is no way for them to fake it.

8. ITC

One lesser-known type of mediumship is known as ITC or instrumental trans communication. This refers to the communication between our world and other realms through technology. ITC mediums use tools like radios, computers, and even televisions to receive messages from the beyond. While many people are skeptical of this type of mediumship, some well-documented cases suggest it is real. For example, in the 1970s, a team of researchers in Switzerland recorded voices from the dead using a tape recorder. In more recent years, ITC mediums have used mobile phones and social media to communicate with the other side. Whether you believe in ITC or not, it is an exciting phenomenon worth exploring.

9. Electronic Voice Phenomenon

Electronic voice phenomenon, or EVP, is a mediumship type involving communication from the beyond through electronic devices. This can include radios, TVs, answering machines, and even cell phones. The voices heard during EVP are typically faint and difficult to understand, but they can occasionally be clear and distinct. Many people believe that EVP is a way for the dead to reach out to the living. There are countless stories of people receiving messages from loved ones who have passed away. While no scientific evidence supports this claim, EVP remains a popular phenomenon, with thousands of people worldwide reporting experiences with it.

10. Evidential Mediumship

Evidential mediumship is one type of mediumship that is focused on providing evidence of life after death. During an evidential mediumship reading, the medium will try to provide specific information about the spirit communicating, such as their name, relationship to the sitter, and what they want to say. The goal of evidential mediumship is to provide comfort and closure to the sitter by proving that life after death exists. If you are looking for a medium specializing in this type of reading, ask about their credentials and experience.

Real Mediums in Our Modern World

Many people today are interested in finding a genuine medium, especially in the modern world, where there is so much skepticism about anything that falls outside the realm of science. Some use Tarot cards or crystal balls, while others may simply go into a trance and allow the spirits to speak through them. Some claim to be able to channel messages from the dead, meaning they can receive messages from beyond the grave.

While it can be challenging to know whether or not a medium is truly gifted, there are certain signs you should look for. A good medium will usually have some kind of information about the person they are communicating with that they could not have otherwise known. They should also be able to provide specific details about the deceased, which others can verify. If you think you may have found a real medium, it is always best to get a second opinion from someone who is experienced in this field.

Scientific Proof

In recent years, there has been an increase in the number of people who claim to be able to contact the dead, and there is scientific evidence that this is indeed possible. One study by the University of Arizona showed that people who spoke to a medium could accurately describe details about their deceased loved ones, even when they had no prior knowledge of those details. This study provides strong evidence for the existence of mediums and their ability to communicate with the other side.

Today, there is a lot of skepticism surrounding the idea of mediums. However, there is also scientific proof that they exist and can communicate with the dead. This proof should be enough to convince even the most skeptical person that mediums are genuine and that they can provide us with valuable information about our loved ones who have passed away.

Mediumship is a centuries-old practice that has been used by people all over the world to communicate with their lost loved ones. There are many different types of mediumship, and each one has its unique way of providing evidence of life after death. While there is still much skepticism surrounding this topic, the increasing amount of scientific proof that mediums are real should be enough to convince even the most skeptical person.

With the help of a real medium, we can obtain closure and comfort by receiving messages from our loved ones who have passed away. This is an invaluable experience that can help us heal after the loss of a loved one. If you are interested in finding a real medium, ask about their credentials and experience. With the help of a gifted medium, you can obtain the closure and peace of mind you need.

Chapter 2: Your Astral Body and the Spirit World

If you are like most people, you have probably wondered what happens to us after we die. What becomes of our spirit? Is there an afterlife? And if so, what is it like? These are some of the questions that mediums seek to answer. Mediumship is the practice of communicating with the spirits of those who have passed on. To do this, mediums must first understand what the spirit is – and what the afterlife is like.

The subtle body is an energy field that surrounds and permeates the physical body.
https://www.pexels.com/photo/white-moon-on-hands-3278643/

According to many belief systems, the spirit is an immortal part of each of us that lives on after the physical body dies. The afterlife is often seen as a place where we can be reunited with our loved ones and enjoy eternal happiness. While there is much we do not yet know about the afterlife, mediums can provide us with valuable insights into this mystery through their unique ability to communicate with the spirits of those who have gone before.

This chapter will explore the nature of the spirit and the afterlife according to mediumship. We will begin by looking at the subtle body, which is often seen as the seat of the soul. We will then explore the astral body, which is believed to be the vehicle that carries our spirit after death. Next, we will examine how different belief systems perceive the soul. Finally, we will take a closer look at the afterlife and how mediums can help us to understand this mystery.

The Subtle Body

Most people are familiar with the physical body, but fewer are aware of the subtle body. The subtle body is an energy field that surrounds and permeates the physical body. It consists of the nadis, or energy channels, through which prana, or life force, flows. The subtle body also contains the chakras, or energy centers, through which prana is circulated.

The subtle body is often seen as the seat of the soul. It is a non-physical body that is believed to interpenetrate and extend beyond the physical body. The subtle body is composed of etheric, emotional, mental, and astral bodies. These bodies are believed to be constantly interacting with each other and the physical body.

The etheric body is the densest of the subtle bodies and is closest to the physical body; it is responsible for our physical health and vitality. The emotional body is composed of our feelings and emotions; it is in constant flux, changing as our emotions change. The mental body is composed of our thoughts and beliefs; it is the bridge between the physical and astral bodies.

Mediumship is the ability to perceive and work with the subtle body. Sensitive people can see the aura, or energy field, around another person. They can also feel the flow of prana in the nadis and chakras. By aligning their energies with those of another person, they can create a bridge between the physical and subtle bodies. This allows them to perceive and transmit messages from one level of consciousness to another. Mediums can also use their abilities to heal imbalances in the subtle body. By clearing blockages and restoring the flow of prana, they can promote physical, emotional, and spiritual wellness.

The Astral Body

According to the belief of mediumship, the soul leaves the physical body and enters into an astral body when people die. This astral body is made up of subtle energy which vibrates at a higher frequency than the physical world. With this astral body, we can travel to different realms and dimensions. There are also different vibration levels within the astral world, which may account for people's different experiences while in this state. For example, some people may only see colors, while others may see detailed landscapes.

The astral body is the lightest and most ethereal of the subtle bodies. It is believed to be our spirit body and the vehicle that carries our spirit after death. In some belief systems, the astral body is also known as the soul body. When we die, the astral body leaves the physical body behind and enters the afterlife. The astral body is often seen as a reflection of our true self. It is the part of us that is eternal and unchanging regardless of the vibration level; the astral world is said to be a place of peace and love. It is also believed that we can communicate with our loved ones who have passed on to the astral world. So next time you're wondering what happens after we die, remember that we may just be entering into another realm where we can explore and discover more about ourselves and the universe around us.

The Connection between the Astral Body and Spirit

Our astral body is our ethereal body; it is the vehicle of our soul and houses our consciousness. The astral body is connected to the physical body by a silver cord. This cord allows us to return to our physical bodies after we die. The astral body can also travel outside the physical body during sleep or in an out-of-body experience. Some people believe that the astral body is our true self and that the physical body is just a shell.

Our astral body contains our memories, thoughts, and feelings. It is made up of our spiritual energy. The astral dimension is a higher vibration than the physical dimension. Our astral body vibrates at a higher frequency than our physical body. This is why we can travel to different planes of existence and interact with other beings on these planes. Our spirit is the part of us that is eternal. It is who we are. Our spirit inhabits our astral body. It is what remains after we die and our physical bodies degrade back into the earth. Our spirit lives on in the spiritual realm.

How Different Practices See the Soul

Though the soul is a difficult concept to define, it is a central tenet of many religious and spiritual traditions. For some, the soul is an immortal essence that transcends the physical body, while others believe it is intimately bound up with our material existence. This varies from one tradition to the next, and there are many different ways of understanding the soul.

In Christianity, the soul is often seen as immortal and separate from the body. This means that when someone dies, their soul goes to either heaven or hell, depending on whether they have been good or bad during their life. In contrast, some Eastern philosophies see the soul as being intimately connected with the body.

Buddhism: The Soul Is Interconnected with All Things

Buddhism believes that we are reborn after death into different bodies, and our consciousness grows and develops over time. The soul is not seen as separate from the body in this tradition but rather as constantly changing and evolving. As you can see, many different understandings of the soul exist, and these differing beliefs can lead to very different practices.

Hinduism: The Soul Is Immanent

In Hinduism, the soul is seen as immanent, which means it is intimately bound up with the physical body. This does not mean that the soul is the same as the body but is a part of the body. The soul is seen as an essential part of our being; without it, we would not be able to function.

The soul is believed to be reborn into different bodies after death. This cycle of birth and death is known as samsara. Hinduism believes that the soul is trapped in samsara because of its desires and attachments. The only way to break free from this cycle is to achieve liberation or moksha. Moksha is a state of complete freedom from the cycle of birth and death.

Spiritualism

For spiritualists, the soul is the immaterial part of a human being that survives after death. This belief is based on the idea that there is more to life than just a physical body and the belief that we are all connected to a higher power. While scientific evidence cannot confirm the existence of the soul, many people find comfort in the idea that their loved ones are still with them in some way after they have passed away.

For spiritualists, the soul is not tied to any particular religion or belief system. Instead, it is a universal force connecting all living beings. This means that everyone has the potential to connect with the soul, regardless of their beliefs. The soul is seen as a source of wisdom and guidance, providing us with a path to follow in life. Ultimately, spiritualists believe that the soul is what makes us truly human and that it is our connection to the divine.

Shamanism

Shamanism is an ancient spiritual practice that has been practiced for centuries by indigenous cultures worldwide. At its core, shamanism is a way to connect with nature and the spirit world to promote healing and balance. Shamans believe everything in the universe is connected and that imbalances in the natural world can lead to illness and disharmony. One of the ways that shamans seek to restore balance is by working with the soul.

According to shamanic belief, the soul consists of three parts; the upper soul, lower soul, and middle soul. The upper soul is responsible for our spiritual connection to the divine, while the lower soul is responsible for our physical needs and desires. The middle soul acts as a bridge between the two, helping us to find harmony and balance in our lives. Shamans believe that when one of these parts of the soul becomes disconnected or imbalanced, it can lead to physical or psychological problems. By working with the soul, shamans can help to restore balance and harmony, promoting wellness on all levels.

Voodoo

In many cultures, the soul is seen as an ethereal entity that exists beyond the physical body. For voodoo practitioners, however, the soul is a very real and tangible force. To them, the soul is not just a spiritual essence but a physical one as well. This belief is based on the idea that the soul is composed of two parts; the *ti bon ange* and the *gros bon ange.*

The ti bon ange is the "little good angel" that resides within every person. It is responsible for our thoughts and emotions, and it is what gives us our individuality. The gros bon ange, on the other hand, is the "big good angel" that resides in the spirit world. It is responsible for our destiny, and it is what allows us to connect with the divine. Together, these two parts of the soul make up our entire being.

Afterlife

The concept of an afterlife has been a topic of discussion and debate for centuries. Some people believe there is life after death, while others contend that death is the end. There is no clear evidence either way, and it largely comes down to personal belief. Many religions have their own beliefs about what happens after death. Christians believe in heaven and hell, while Buddhists believe in reincarnation. There is no right or wrong answer, which ultimately comes down to each individual's beliefs. After all, we all have to die eventually, so it makes sense to think about what happens afterward. Regardless of what anyone believes, the concept of an afterlife will continue to be a source of fascination for centuries to come.

What Is the Afterlife?

The idea of an afterlife has been a source of comfort and hope for people throughout history. In many cultures, the belief in some form of life after death is central to religious teachings. For those who adhere to these beliefs, the afterlife is often seen as a place of reward or punishment, depending on their actions during this life. While the specifics may differ, the general idea is that the soul survives the body's death and goes on to another realm.

What that realm looks like is a matter of speculation, but it is often described as a paradise-like environment or a hellish one. Some believe there is reincarnation, while others hold that there is simply an end to consciousness. Whatever the case may be, the belief in an afterlife provides comfort for many in the face of death.

What Happens to Spirits When We Die?

There are many different beliefs about what happens to spirits when we die, but the one thing that everyone can agree on is that death is a mystery. Some believe that spirits go to a peaceful place where they can rest and watch over their loved ones. Others believe that spirits are reincarnated and come back as different people or animals. And still, others believe that spirits simply cease to exist after death. While we may never know for sure what happens to spirits when we die, it's comforting to know that there are many different beliefs about the afterlife. Whatever your beliefs may be, remember that death is a natural part of life, and there is no need to be afraid of it. Instead, embrace it as a part of the cycle of life and death.

Afterlife in Spiritualism

Spiritualists believe that the soul lives on after the physical body dies and that communication with the dead is possible. Proponents of this belief system often hold séances or use other forms of divination to connect with deceased loved ones. While some may view spiritualism as a way to scam unsuspecting people, many believe it is a legitimate way to connect with the other side. After all, if we have souls that live on after death, it stands to reason that they want to communicate with us. Whether or not you believe in spiritualism, it is an interesting way to think about the afterlife.

Afterlife in Shamanism

In shamanism, the afterlife is often seen as a journey through different realms. The soul is believed to travel to the underworld, facing challenges and transforming. After completing these trials, the soul is reborn into the spiritual world and given a new life. This cycle of death and rebirth is thought to continue until the soul reaches a state of enlightenment. Some shamans also believe it is possible to communicate with the dead, and they often use trance states to contact spirits in the spirit world. By understanding the afterlife, shamans can help their clients to make peace with death and prepare for their spiritual journey.

Afterlife in Voodoo Culture

In Voodoo culture, there is a strong belief in the afterlife. This belief is rooted in the idea that the soul is immortal and that it will continue to exist even after the body has died. The soul is seen as being locked inside the body, and it is only when the body dies that the soul can be released. Once released, the soul goes on to live in another realm known as the spirit world. In this world, the soul will be reunited with its ancestors and will be able to enjoy eternal happiness. The concept of reincarnation also plays a role in Voodoo's beliefs about the afterlife. It is believed that the soul can be reborn into another body and that this process will continue until the soul has attained perfection. Because of this, death is not seen as an ending but rather as a new beginning.

Peeking into the Afterlife

Most people have at least some curiosity about what happens after we die. It's only natural to wonder about the great unknown. Unfortunately, there's no way to know for sure what happens to us after we die. But that doesn't stop people from speculating. For many people, the thought of peeking into the afterlife is both intriguing and terrifying. It's an essential part of the human experience and helps us appreciate life all the more.

Many people believe that the afterlife is a mystery. Still, some say that it is possible to peek into the afterlife to find answers. Mediums are often able to communicate with the dead, and they may be able to provide information about what happens after death. While it is impossible to know for sure what happens after we die, talking to a medium may give you some peace of mind about what lies ahead. If you are curious about the afterlife, consider talking to a medium. They may just have the answers you are looking for.

The idea of mediumship – communicating with the dead – has been around for centuries. In recent years, however, it has become far more mainstream, thanks in part to shows like "Medium" and "The Long Island Medium." While some people are still skeptical about the validity of mediumship, many have had firsthand experience with the afterlife through the messages delivered by mediums.

For those who have lost loved ones, mediumship can provide much-needed closure. It can be difficult to come to terms with the fact that someone is no longer physically present in our lives. However, a message from beyond the grave can help to ease the pain of loss and provide comfort that our loved ones are still with us, even if we cannot see them.

In addition to providing comfort, mediumship can offer insights into the afterlife. What happens to us after we die? It is a question that has long intrigued people of all faiths. While there are many different beliefs about what happens to us after death, mediums who have communicated with the dead often report similar experiences. This suggests that there may be some truth to what they are saying.

Whether you believe in mediumship or not, it is impossible to deny that it has profoundly impacted many people's lives. For those who have suffered a loss, it can provide much-needed closure. For those curious about the afterlife, it can offer a glimpse into what may lie beyond this life. Whether you are a skeptic or a believer, mediumship is something worth exploring.

The astral body is a part of the human soul that is believed to be capable of traveling outside the physical body. It is connected to the spirit world and is said to be the source of our dreams and intuition. Mediums are people who can communicate with the dead and may be able to provide information about the afterlife. The idea of mediumship has been around for centuries, but it has become far more mainstream in recent years.

For those who have lost loved ones, mediumship can provide much-needed closure. It can also offer insights into the afterlife for those curious about what happens to us after we die. Whether you believe in mediumship or not, it is something worth exploring. Talking to a medium may give you peace of mind about what lies ahead. If you are curious about the afterlife, consider talking to a medium. They may just have the answers you are looking for.

Chapter 3: Grounding and Preparation

If you've ever been interested in mediumship, you know that it's not as simple as just talking to ghosts. A lot of preparation and work goes into it, both on the part of the medium and the person seeking to communicate with a loved one who has passed away. Without proper grounding and preparation, it's too easy to get caught up in the spiritual world without being able to control the situation or protect yourself from negative entities.

When it comes to mediumship, grounding and preparation are extremely essential.
https://www.pexels.com/photo/woman-in-white-shirt-holding-orange-and-white-lollipop-6943953/

In this chapter, we'll talk about the importance of grounding and preparation for mediumship. We will also discuss some simple but effective grounding exercises you can do to get started. We'll focus on the medium's side of things. Still, many of these tips can be applied to anyone looking to improve their connection with the "beyond." We'll also discuss ways to prepare your mind so that you're more receptive to messages from the other side.

The Importance of Grounding and Preparation

Mediumship is a skill that has been practiced for centuries, and it only recently began to gain mainstream acceptance. Despite its growing popularity, mediumship is still shrouded in mystery. Many people are unsure how to prepare for readings or what to expect. One of the most crucial things to remember is that mediumship is two-way communication.

The medium acts as a conduit between the physical and spiritual worlds. Still, it is up to the spirit to decide whether or not they want to communicate. This is why it is so essential to be properly prepared before readings. Grounding yourself will help you to feel more anchored and connected, making it easier for spirits to reach you. And taking some time to relax and clear your mind will make it easier for you to receive messages from the other side.

When it comes to mediumship, grounding and preparation are extremely essential. Here are some reasons why:

1. Helps You Stay Focused

As a medium, it is vital to be well-grounded and prepared before you begin readings. Grounding yourself will help you feel more connected to the physical world and prevent you from becoming overwhelmed by spirit energy. There are many different ways to ground yourself. Still, some common methods include visualizing roots growing from your feet into the earth or holding a piece of quartz in your hand. Once you feel firmly grounded, you can begin preparing for your reading. This may involve setting an intention, visualizing a protective bubble around yourself, or calling in your spirit guides. Taking the time to ground and prepare yourself before beginning a reading will help you stay focused and attuned to the messages you receive.

2. Increases Your Chances of Making Contact

Grounding yourself will help you feel more centered, making it easier to focus your mind and connect with the energies of the spirit world. Preparation is also important, as it helps to clear your mind of any negative thoughts or emotions that could block your connection. When you are properly prepared, you are more likely to contact the spirit you seek to communicate with. It becomes easier for them to reach you and easier for you to receive their messages. By taking the time to ground and prepare yourself before a session, you'll increase your chances of making contact with the spirit world and receiving accurate messages.

3. Improves Your Connection

When it comes to mediumship, grounding and preparation are key to establishing a strong connection with the spirit world. Taking the time to ground yourself before you begin readings will help you clear your mind and focus your energy. This will allow you to be more receptive to the messages the spirit is trying to communicate. Similarly, preparing for readings by setting an intention and creating a sacred space can also help you connect more deeply with your guides and loved ones who have passed on. By taking the time to create a strong foundation, you'll be sure to get the most out of your mediumship reading.

4. Keeps You Safe from Negative Entities

As a medium, being well-grounded and prepared before you start to work will protect you from any negative entities that may try to attach themselves to you. There are a few simple things that you can do to make sure that you are safe before you begin readings. First, set the intention that only positive and highest good can come through. This will keep out any lower energies trying to attach themselves to you. Secondly, call in your spirit guides and ask them to surround and protect you. You can also imagine a white light surrounding you, creating a protective barrier against any negative energy.

Always say a prayer or meditate before you start working. This will help to raise your vibration levels and keep you in a positive state of mind. Wearing protective clothing such as a white robe or pendant will create a barrier between you and any negative energy. Finally, always work in a clean and clutter-free space. This will help create a calm and safe environment for you to work in. These simple tips can keep you safe from negative entities when working as a medium.

5. Helps You Manage Your Energy

Grounding yourself before you begin readings will help you to manage your energy and prevent you from becoming overwhelmed by the spirit world. When properly grounded, you can work more effectively as a medium and avoid burnout. Remember that you don't have to be always available to the spirit world. You can take breaks when you need to and return to your readings when you feel more centered.

Grounding Exercises

Mediumship grounding is a technique used to help mediums connect with the spirit world while remaining grounded in the physical world. The goal is to create a bridge between the two worlds so that communication can flow freely. There are many different ways to ground oneself. Still, some of the most common methods include visualization, meditation, and energy work.

When done properly, grounding can help to prevent psychic overload and promote clear and accurate communication with spirits. Not all mediums are the same, so finding a grounding method that works best for you is crucial. With practice, you'll be able to achieve a deeper connection with the spirit world while remaining fully present in the physical world.

1. The Tree Method

Many people new to mediumship are unaware of the different ways of grounding. One easy way to ground yourself is to imagine roots growing from the soles of your feet, anchoring you to the earth. Another method is to imagine yourself as a tree, with your feet rooted firmly in the ground and your arms reaching up toward the sky. This exercise can be done anywhere and only takes a few minutes. It is a great way to center yourself before beginning readings and can also be used to release excess energy after a session. Give it a try the next time you are feeling scattered or ungrounded.

2. The Balloon Method

There are several different exercises you can do to help you practice grounding. One such exercise is known as the balloon method. To try it out, sit comfortably and take a few deep breaths. Then, imagine that you are holding a balloon in your hand. Once you have a clear image of the balloon, mentally inflate it until it is about the size of a grapefruit. As you do so, mentally repeat the words, "I am expanding my mediumship abilities." Once the balloon is inflated, visualize it floating up into the air and then popping. As it does, feel your mediumship abilities expanding. This exercise can be done as often as you like, and with practice, you'll find that it becomes easier and more effective. Who knows – with enough practice, you may just be able to pop that balloon without even using your hands!

3. The Stone Method

Another simple way to ground yourself is with a stone. Start by finding a stone that feels comfortable to hold. It can be any size or shape, and it should be smooth so that it's easy to hold. Once you have your stone, sit down in a comfortable position and close your eyes. Take a few deep breaths and focus on the feel of the stone in your hand. Imagine roots growing from the stone and anchoring you to the earth. Visualize the roots going deep into the ground, spreading outward, and holding you securely in place.

As you focus on the roots, you should feel yourself becoming more grounded and present in the physical world. If you start feeling lightheaded or dizzy, open your eyes and take a few deep breaths until you feel better. Once you're grounded, you can put the stone down and continue your day. Grounding exercises like this one can help to protect you from negative energies and prevent you from becoming overwhelmed during a reading.

4. The Earthing Method

If you've ever felt disconnected, spaced out, or "not all there," it could be that you're not properly grounded. To remedy this, try the earthing method. Sit or stand with your feet planted firmly on the ground, and imagine roots growing from the soles of your feet deep into the earth below. Visualize these roots anchoring you to the planet, and focus on the sensation of being solidly connected. You should feel more present and focused after just a few minutes. If you don't have time to do a full grounding exercise, simply take a few deep breaths and visualize your feet rooted to the ground. This will help to center and ground you so that you can fully engage with the world around you.

5. The Visualization Method

One of the most effective methods to ground yourself is the visualization method. To do this exercise, find a comfortable place to sit or lie down. Close your eyes and take a few deep breaths. Visualize that a bright white light surrounds you. This light is cleansing and purifying, and it surrounds you with protection.

As you breathe in, imagine that you are taking in the earth's energy. Continue to breathe deeply and visualize the energy entering your body and filling you up. You should feel more grounded and connected to the earth with each breath. Feel the earth's energy entering your body and filling you with strength and stability. Open your eyes and continue with your readings when you feel well grounded.

Ways to Prepare Your Mind

If you're interested in developing your mediumship skills, you need to prepare your mind. It's a good idea to keep an open mind and be open to the possibility of receiving messages from beyond. However, it's also crucial to be mindful of your thoughts and emotions. These negative emotions will block you from receiving messages if you feel doubtful, scared, or anxious. Finding a balance between being open-minded and maintaining positive thoughts is essential. There are a few things you can do to prepare your mind for a reading:

1. Meditation

Suppose you're interested in developing your mediumship skills. In that case, one of the best things you can do is learn how to meditate. It can help to still your mind and open your consciousness, making it easier to receive psychic impressions from the spirit world. There are many different ways to meditate, so experiment until you find a method that works for you.

Some people prefer to sit or lie in a quiet place, focusing on their breath and letting their thoughts come and go without judgment. Others prefer to focus on a mantra or visualize a white light surrounding them. There is no right or wrong way to meditate. Find a practice that helps you to relax and open your mind. Regular meditation can help you to develop your mediumistic abilities and strengthen your connection to the spirit world.

2. Visualization

Visualization is one of the best ways to prepare your mind for mediumship. It is the process of creating mental images in your mind to achieve a specific goal. When you visualize, you use your imagination to create an image of what you want to happen. For example, if you want to communicate with a loved one who has passed away, you would visualize the two of you talking and sharing memories. The more realistic and detailed the image, the better.

The goal is to create a clear picture in your mind so that when you enter into mediumship, you'll be able to see and hear your loved one more clearly. Visualization has many other benefits, such as reducing stress and increasing your overall well-being. If you are new to visualization, start practicing daily for a few minutes. As you become more comfortable with the practice, you can increase the time you spend visualizing.

3. Affirmations

If you're interested in developing your mediumship skills, you can do a few things to prepare your mind. One of the most important is to practice affirmations. This involves repeating positive statements about your ability to connect with the other side. For example, you might say, "I am a gifted medium who can communicate with those who have passed on." By regularly repeating these affirmations, you'll begin to increase your self-confidence and belief in your abilities. This will make it easier for you to relax and open yourself up to the spirit world.

In addition to affirmations, another helpful way to prepare your mind for mediumship is to meditate while affirming positive thoughts. This will help you to still your thoughts and achieve a state of inner peace. When you can quieten your mind, it will be easier to receive messages from the other side. Be open-minded and receptive to the possibility of communicating with spirits. If you approach mediumship with skepticism or doubt, it will be more difficult to receive clear messages. Following these simple tips can set you up for success as a medium.

4. Prayer

Praying is one of the most crucial things you can do to prepare your mind for mediumship. Prayer quiets the mind and clears away any distracting thoughts. It also helps to open the heart, making it more receptive to communication from the Spirits. When praying, imagine yourself surrounded by light. Picture the light expanding until it fills your entire being. Sense the light infusing you with peace, love, and strength. Let go of all your fears and doubts, and allow yourself to be filled with the light of Spirit. As you do so, you'll find it easier to quieten your mind and open your heart to communication from the other side.

5. Connecting with Nature

Connecting with nature is one of the most effective ways to get into the right mindset. Spend time surrounded by plants and trees, and take in the beauty of the natural world. This will help you to quiet your mind and focus your thoughts. You might also want to try meditating or doing some deep-breathing exercises. These activities will help still your mind and allow you to receive guidance from the other side. Remember, the key is to relax and allow yourself to be open to the experience. With a little practice, you'll be surprised at what you're able to accomplish.

6. Keeping an Open Mind

When getting your mind ready for mediumship, it is vital to have an open perspective. Throughout history, many people have been skeptical of mediumship and the ability to communicate with the dead. However, remember that mediumship is a natural ability that we all possess. Just as we can use our five senses to interact with the physical world, we can also use our sixth sense to interact with the spiritual world. With an open mind, you'll be able to more easily receive messages from your loved ones who have passed on. In addition, you'll also be more receptive to messages from your spirit guide. Keep an open mind, and you'll be well on your way to becoming a successful medium.

7. Trusting Your Intuition

To prepare your mind for the experience, learn to trust your intuition. Intuition is our inner guidance system and is often the first step in receiving psychic information. To develop it, it's crucial to quiet your mind and get in touch with your feelings. Meditation can be a helpful tool for this, but simply taking some time each day to focus on your breath can also be helpful. It's also essential to pay attention to the messages you receive from your body. Our bodies often give us information about people and situations before our minds do. By learning to trust your intuition, you'll open yourself up to a new world of psychic experiences.

8. Yoga

You've probably heard of yoga before, but did you know that it can also be used to prepare your mind for mediumship? It is an ancient practice that involves physical, mental, and spiritual disciplines. The physical aspect of yoga involves stretching and strengthening the body. In contrast, the mental and spiritual aspects involve breathwork and meditation. By focusing on the breath and clearing the mind of all other thoughts, yoga can help to still the mind and create a sense of inner peace. This state of mind is ideal for mediumship as it makes connecting with the spirit world easier. In addition, it can also help to develop psychic abilities and expand your consciousness. So if you're looking for a way to prepare your mind for mediumship, yoga might be the perfect option for you.

When engaging in mediumship, it is critical to be properly grounded and have your mind focused on the task at hand. Grounding yourself will help to protect you from outside influences and clear your mind of any unwanted thoughts or distractions. You can ground yourself by visualizing roots growing from your feet and anchoring you to the earth. Once you are grounded, prepare your mind for the session. This can be done through meditation or visualization exercises. It is also crucial to take some time to connect with nature. Spend a few minutes focusing on your breath and taking in the peace and beauty of your surroundings. By taking these steps, you'll receive accurate messages during your session and be better able to focus.

Chapter 4: How to Recognize Energy

Have you ever walked into a room and felt an instant connection or disconnection with the people in it? Have you ever been able to sense the energy of a person or place just by being near it? If so, then you may have already experienced the act of sensing energy.

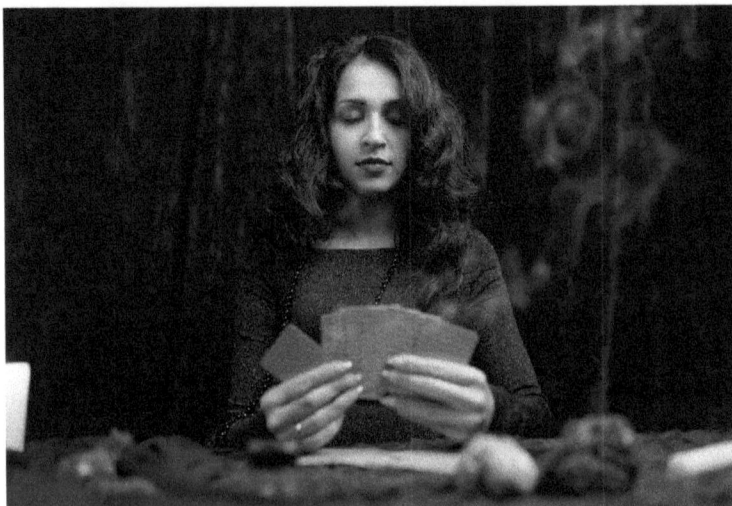

Mediums can open themselves up to seeing and communicating with the spirit world.
https://www.pexels.com/photo/woman-doing-a-card-reading-8770834/

In mediumship, recognizing and understanding the energy around you can be extremely helpful when it comes to discerning the difference between a deceased loved one and a lower-vibrational entity. It can also help you understand the messages you receive. The energy of a person or place can tell you a lot about what they are thinking or feeling at any given moment.

There are many different ways to sense energy. Some people are more naturally attuned to sensing energy than others, but with a little practice, anyone can learn how to do it. This chapter will teach you how to visualize and sense energy on your own and with others. It will also provide you with some exercises you can practice to develop your ability to sense energy.

How to Visualize and Sense Energy

Visualizing and sensing energy are two important skills for anyone interested in mediumship. Through visualization, mediums can open themselves up to seeing and communicating with the spirit world. By sensing energy, mediums can interpret the emotions and thoughts of spirits. These abilities require practice and concentration, but they can be developed with time and patience. Sensing energy is a skill that takes time and practice to develop. The more you practice, the better you'll become at it. Here are some tips to help you develop your ability to visualize and sense energy:

1. Relax and Open Your Mind

The ability to see and feel energy is a skill that anyone can learn. However, it does take some practice to develop this ability. The first step is to relax and clear your mind. It is crucial to be in a state of relaxation to sense energy. Once you are relaxed, start to focus on your breath. Take slow, deep breaths and allow your mind to become calm and still. Once you have reached a state of inner peace, start to visualize energy. See it swirling around you, filling the space with its bright light. Feel the energy flowing through your body, energizing and revitalizing you. With practice, you'll develop the ability to sense energy more clearly. Eventually, you'll be able to see and feel the energy all around you, anytime and anywhere.

2. Look for a Change in Your Environment

One way to tell if there is an energy change in your environment is to see if the space around you feels different. For example, if you walk into a room that feels heavy or dense, there may be negative energy.

Alternatively, if a space feels light and airy, it may be because the energy is positive. Another way to sense energy is to *focus on your body.* If you suddenly feel tense or uncomfortable, it may be because negative energy is nearby. On the other hand, if you feel relaxed and at ease, it could be because the energy in your environment is positive.

3. Pay Attention to Your Physical Sensations

One way to become more attuned to energy is to pay attention to your physical sensations. For example, you might notice that you feel lighter when you are in the presence of positive energy and heavier or constricted when you are around negative energy. You might also notice changes in your breathing, heart rate, or tingling sensation. These are just some of the ways your body can respond to different kinds of energy. By paying attention to your physical sensations, you can begin to get a sense of the different energy types around you.

4. Notice How You Feel Emotionally and Mentally

You may not see energy, but you can most certainly feel it. Energy is everywhere, and it affects us in both subtle and profound ways. Learning how to visualize and sense energy can help us understand our own emotions and mental state, as well as the energies of others. When we pay attention to how we feel emotionally and mentally, we can begin to get a sense of the energy around us. Pay attention to your emotions and thoughts. If you feel angry or anxious for no reason, it could be because of an energetic imbalance. However, if you feel happy and peaceful, it may be because the energy around you is supportive. By paying attention to these signs, you can get a better sense of the energy in your environment.

6. Trust Your Intuition

Energy is all around us, but it can be hard to sense and visualize. Some people seem to have a natural ability to see and feel the energy, while others find it more difficult. However, there are some things that you can do to help yourself become more attuned to the energy around you. One of the most essential things is to trust your intuition. If you get a feeling or see something in your mind's eye, don't second-guess yourself – go with it. It's also helpful to spend time in nature, where you can feel the energy flow around you. And finally, don't be afraid to experiment. There are many different ways to sense and see energy, so try out different techniques until you find one that works. With a little practice, you'll be amazed at how much easier it is to connect with the world of energy that surrounds us all.

7. Practice, Practice, Practice!

Learning how to visualize and sense energy is a skill that takes time and practice to develop. The first step is to simply become aware of the energy around you. Start by focusing on objects in your environment and notice the energy they emit. Once you become more attuned to the energy around you, you can experiment with ways of manipulating it. For example, try holding your hands a few inches apart and focusing on the energy flow between them. Keep practicing until you develop a stronger sense of how energy works and how it can be used to improve your health and well-being.

Exercises for Sensing One's Energy

Energy is all around us. It's in the air we breathe, the food we eat, and the water we drink. It's also in the people we interact with and the places we visit. Our bodies are made up of energy, and our thoughts and emotions are also forms of energy. We constantly interact with energy, whether or not we are aware of it. One way to become more aware of it is to learn how to sense your energy field. This can be done through various methods, including meditation, visualization, and breathwork. By taking the time to sense your energy, you can become more attuned to the energy around you. Doing so can teach you how to better manage it and create a more positive and balanced life. Here are some exercises to help you get started:

1. The Ball of Light Exercise

You can learn to sense your energy even if you can't see it. One way to do this is through the "ball of light" exercise. First, find a comfortable place to sit or lie down. Close your eyes and take a few deep breaths. Then, imagine a ball of light inside your chest. It can be any color or size that you choose. Spend a few minutes focusing on the ball of light, and pay attention to any sensations that you feel in your body. You may feel warmth, tingling, or pulsing. The more you focus on the ball of light, the stronger these sensations will become. With practice, you'll be able to sense your energy more and more clearly.

2. The Rope Exercise

We're all empathic beings, capable of sensing the energy of those around us. And while it's a skill that can be useful in many situations, it can also be overwhelming if we're not used to it. One way to start learning how to control your ability to sense energy is by doing the rope exercise.

The rope exercise is simple. Find a partner and stand facing each other, about an arm's length apart. Take turns holding one end of a rope while your partner holds the other. Then, try to communicate your energy to your partner through the rope without speaking. Focus on sending calm or happy energy, and see if they can receive it. You may be surprised at how well it works! With practice, you'll be able to better control your abilities and use them in more helpful ways rather than overwhelming.

3. The Scanning Exercise

The scanning exercise is an easy way to train yourself to be more aware of your energy. To begin, find a comfortable place to sit or lie down. Close your eyes and take a few deep breaths, allowing your body to relax. Once you feel calm, focus your attention on your breath. Inhale deeply, and then exhale slowly. As you breathe, imagine you are drawing in energy from the air around you. This energy will fill your body, infusing every cell with vitality.

Once you feel filled with energy, begin to scan your body from head to toe. Notice how this energy feels as it flows through you. Pay attention to any areas where the energy feels particularly strong or weak. With practice, you'll develop a greater sensitivity to the flow of energy within your own body. This exercise can be done anywhere, at any time, making it easy to cultivate your ability to sense energy. By learning to sense your energy, you'll be better positioned to detect and understand the energy of others.

4. The Ray of Light Exercise

We are all energy beings and constantly interact with the energy around us. Just like we tune into different channels on a TV, we can tune into different energy frequencies. When we tune into a high frequency, we feel good. We feel happy, joyful, and at ease. When we tune into a low frequency, we feel bad. We feel angry, sad, and anxious. Learning to sense energy can help us to avoid negative people and situations and attract more of what we want into our lives.

The Ray of Light exercise is one method to practice sensing energy. First, find a comfortable place to sit or lie down. Close your eyes and take a few deep breaths. Then imagine a ray of light shining down from the sky and hitting you in the center of your forehead. The light will enter your body and fill you with positive energy. As you breathe in, feel the light expanding throughout your body. Fill your entire being with the light until you radiate positive energy. Now open your eyes and notice how you feel. You should feel lighter, brighter, and more at peace. With practice, you'll be able to sense energy anywhere, anytime!

5. The Crystal Ball Exercise

One of the best ways to get in touch with your energy is to do the crystal ball exercise. This exercise is simple and only takes a few minutes. To begin, sit comfortably and hold a crystal ball in your hands. Close your eyes and take a few deep breaths. Imagine that your breath is filling the crystal ball with light as you breathe. Once the ball is filled up, imagine it emanating from the center and moving outward in all directions. Continue to breathe deeply and focus on the light until you feel yourself becoming calm and relaxed.

Now, imagine that you are looking into the crystal ball and that it is showing you images of your energy. Observe the color, shape, and movement of the energy in the ball. Spend a few minutes observing your energy before opening your eyes. When you have finished, take a few deep breaths and write down what you saw in the crystal ball. This exercise is a great way to get in touch with your energy and learn more about how it affects your everyday life.

6. The Grounding Exercise

We must learn how to sense and connect with our energy to live healthy, happy lives. The grounding exercise is one way to help improve your focus. To begin, find a comfortable place to sit or stand. Close your eyes and take a few deep breaths. As you inhale, imagine roots growing down from your feet into the earth. With each exhale, feel yourself becoming more rooted and grounded.

Allow yourself to sink deeply into the earth. Imagine its energy coming up through your roots and into your body. Breathe in this nourishing energy and let it fill you up. When you're ready, open your eyes and take a few minutes to notice how you feel. You should feel more connected to the earth and more centered within yourself. With practice, you'll be able to access this feeling anytime, anywhere.

7. The Centering Exercise

Most people are unaware of the energy they exude. We go about our days not sensing the effect we have on those around us. However, this energy is very real and can be harnessed to create positive outcomes in our lives. You can get in touch with your energy by doing the centering exercise. Start by closing your eyes and taking a few deep breaths. Then, focus on your hands and imagine a white light emanating from them. This light represents your energy.

Now, bring your hands slowly up to your chest and imagine the light entering your heart space. As you do this, you should feel a sense of calm and relaxation wash over you. Continue to breathe deeply and focus on the light until you feel fully centered. This exercise can be done anytime you need to connect with your energy and center yourself.

Sensing Others' Energy

Many experts believe that we are all connected by an invisible energy field. This field is often referred to as the "aura." Some people can see the aura, while others can sense it. Sensing the aura of others is sometimes called "auric sensing." There are many different ways to sense someone else's energy. For some people, it may be a physical feeling, like warmth or tingling in the body. Others may get a mental or emotional sense of the person's energy. And some people may see colors or shapes around the person.

If you think you may be sensing other people's energy, you can do a few things to develop your ability. With practice, you may find that you're able to sense the energy of others more clearly. And who knows? You may even discover that you have a hidden talent for auric sensing. Here are a few things you can do to develop your ability to sense others' energy:

1. The Mirror Exercise

We are all walking around with our energy field or aura. You may not be able to see it, but you can feel it. When you walk into a room, you can sense the energy of the people around you. Some people have calm, soothing energy, while others have high energy, which is almost overwhelming. Have you ever walked into a room and felt instantly uncomfortable? That is because you were picking up on the negative energy of the people around you.

Fortunately, there is a way to protect yourself from negative energy and even start to influence the energy of the people around you. It's called the mirror exercise, and it is a simple but powerful tool for sensing and managing energy. The exercise is exactly what it sounds like - you stand in front of a mirror and imagine your aura reflecting on you. As you look at your reflection, imagine your aura is strong and bright. Visualize your energy being so strong that it fills up the entire mirror. Now, imagine that the people around you are reflecting their energy field. See their auras filling up the space around them. Finally, imagine that your aura is so powerful that it starts to influence the energy of the people around you, making them calmer and more positive.

The mirror exercise is a great way to get in touch with your energy field and start to manage the energy of the people around you. Give it a try next time you walk into a room full of people and see how it makes you feel.

2. The Empathy Exercise

By becoming more attuned to the energy around us, we can learn to protect our positive energy and prevent it from being drained. That's what the empathy exercise is all about. The first step is finding a quiet place to relax and clear your mind. Once you're calm, start paying attention to the people around you. Notice how their energy makes you feel. Are you feeling happy and upbeat, or are you feeling tired and down?

If you start to feel negative after being around someone, it's a good sign that their energy is negatively affecting you. In this case, it's best to try to avoid them. However, if you're drawn to someone's positive energy, then, by all means, talk to them! By practicing this exercise, you can become more attuned to the energies around you and learn to protect your positive energy.

3. The Cord-Cutting Exercise

Negative energy can be contagious, but so can positive energy. The key is to surround yourself with people who have positive energy and avoid those who drain you. That's where the cord-cutting exercise comes in. This exercise is designed to help you break free from the negative energy of others so that you can surround yourself with positive people.

To perform the cord-cutting exercise, imagine a bright white light surrounding you. This light is your protection from negative energy.

Now, imagine that you are surrounded by people who drain your energy. See their negative energy as dark cords attached to you and draining you. Now, use your imagination to cut these cords. See the cords being cut and falling away from you. As you do that, you'll feel your energy shift and change. You'll feel lighter and more positive. Finally, imagine that you are surrounded by people who have positive energy. See their bright light shining around you. Their positive energy fills you up and makes you happy and healthy.

The cord-cutting exercise is a great way to break free from the negative energy of others and surround yourself with positive people. Give it a try and see how it makes you feel.

By learning to sense and manage energy, you can protect yourself from negative energy and even start to influence the people around you. These exercises are just a starting point. The more you practice, the better you'll become at managing your energy and that of others. So don't be afraid to experiment and see what works best for you. And remember, the more positive energy you put into the world, the more you'll get in return!

Chapter 5: Developing Clairvoyance and Other Clairs

Have you ever wished you could see into the future? Hear what someone is thinking? Or just know things you never did before? If so, then you may be interested in developing your mediumship skills.

Clairvoyance is the ability to see spirits.
https://www.pexels.com/photo/hands-over-fortune-telling-crystal-ball-7179800/

Mediumship is the ability to communicate with the spirits of those who have passed on; it is a skill anyone can learn. There are different ways to develop your mediumship skills. Still, one of the most crucial things is learning to use your clairvoyance, clairaudience, clairsentience, and Claircognizance. This chapter will explore what each of these clairs entails and how you can develop them. By the end of this chapter, you'll have plenty of tools and knowledge to use your mediumship skills in everyday life!

The Four Clairs

The Four Clairs are four ways we can receive information from the spiritual realm. Clairvoyance is the ability to see spirits, clairaudience is the ability to hear them, clairsentience is the ability to feel or sense them, and Claircognizance is the ability to know and understand them. We all have these abilities, but some are more attuned to one or two of them. For example, you may be a clairvoyant who sees images or symbols when you meditate or a clairaudient who hears voices or music. Or you may be a clairsentient who feels energy or emotions or a claircognizant who just knows things. These are all valid ways to receive information from spirits, and there is no right or wrong way to do it. The vital thing is to be open to whatever form of communication comes through for you. Let's explore each of the four clairs in more depth.

Clairvoyance (What to Expect When You're Clairvoyant)

Clairvoyance is the ability to see beyond the five physical senses. Clairvoyant people may see colors and shapes representing people, events, or messages from the other side. Clairvoyance is often associated with psychic ability, but it is important to note that not all psychics are clairvoyant. Some clairvoyants may also have other abilities, such as clairaudience (clear hearing) or clairsentience (clear feeling). Clairvoyant people may see images in their mind's eye, or they may see actual physical objects. Some people report seeing auras around people, while others say they see symbols or flashes of light. This ability can be helpful in many areas of life, from careers to relationships. Many resources are available to help you develop and understand your gift if you think you may be clairvoyant. The most important thing is to trust your intuition and follow your heart.

How to Develop Clairvoyance

Everyone has clairvoyant abilities, but most people are unaware of them or do not know how to develop them. There are many ways to develop clairvoyance, but the most crucial thing is to have an open mind and be willing to explore your abilities.

One way to develop clairvoyance is through intuition. Intuition is an inner knowing that comes from the subconscious mind. We all have intuition, but many of us do not listen to it. To develop your intuition, start by paying attention to your gut feelings. If you get a feeling about something, take some time to investigate it further. You may be surprised at what you find.

Another way to develop clairvoyance is through synchronicities. Synchronicities are meaningful coincidences that cannot be explained by logic or chance. They often occur when we think about someone or something, and they suddenly appear in our lives. For example, you may be thinking about a friend and then run into them at the grocery store. These coincidences are a sign that the universe is trying to get our attention. Pay attention to them and see where they lead you.

Finally, another way to develop clairvoyance is through visions. Visions are glimpses of the future that come to us in our dreams or meditation. To interpret your visions, keep a dream journal and write down any strange or significant dreams you have. You may also want to try meditation or guided visualization exercises. As you practice accessing your psychic abilities, you'll see more clearly in the spiritual realm.

Tips to Improve Clairvoyance

If you are interested in improving your clairvoyant abilities, you can do a few things to speed up the process.

- **Practice Daily:** The more you practice using your abilities, the stronger they will become. Spend some time practicing visualization exercises or working with a psychic medium each day.

- **Get a Reading:** A professional psychic reading can give you some insight into your abilities and what you should be working on.

- **Join a Development Circle:** Many development circles or groups meet regularly to help people develop their abilities. This is a great way to meet other like-minded people and learn from more experienced psychics.

- **Keep a Journal:** Journaling is a great way to track your progress and document your experiences. Write down any dreams, visions, or synchronicities you have.

Clairaudience (What to Expect When You're Clairaudient)

Clairaudience is the ability to hear spirit. This can manifest in many ways, from hearing an inner voice guiding you to hearing sounds like music or laughter. You may even receive messages from Spirit through words or phrases. Clairaudience is often one of the first psychic abilities to develop, and it's a skill that can be used in many different ways. For example, you can use clairaudience to communicate with your Spirit Guides to receive guidance from them on your life path. You can also use clairaudience to connect with loved ones who have passed on and to receive messages from them.

Clairaudience in Everyday Life

Clairaudience can manifest in several ways, from hearing the sounds of nature to receiving messages from the other side. As you develop your clairaudient abilities, you may start to notice that you can more easily remember your dreams. You may also find that you are drawn to certain sounds, such as the sound of running water or birdsong. Clairaudience can also be used to tune into your higher self. By listening for guidance from within, you can begin to make choices that are in alignment with your true desires. With practice, clairaudience can be a powerful tool for accessing inner wisdom and guidance.

How to Develop Clairaudience

Clairaudience is the ability to hear voices and sounds that are not audible to the human ear. These sounds can come from either the spirit world or your higher self. Suppose you are interested in developing this ability. In that case, you can do a few things to open yourself up to the possibility. First, it is important to have an open mind and be receptive to the idea that you may be able to hear things beyond the physical world. Second, try practicing with a friend or medium already attuned to clairaudience. This will help you become more comfortable with the experience.

Finally, try automatic writing. This technique allows your hand to move freely across a sheet of paper without consciously thinking about what you are writing. The words that come through may not make immediate sense, but over time, you may start to see patterns and messages meant for you. Clairaudience is a fascinating ability that can help you connect with the unseen world around you. You may be surprised at what you can hear with a little practice.

Tips for Improving Clairaudience

- **Meditation:** Meditation is a great way to quieten the mind down and open it up to the possibility of hearing the spirit.

- **Relaxation:** Be relaxed when you are trying to develop your clairaudient abilities. Try to find a quiet place where you will not be interrupted.

- **Visualization:** Visualization can be helpful when you are trying to hear spirit. Picturing yourself in a peaceful place, surrounded by nature, can help you attune to the frequency of the spirit.

- **Get in Touch with Your Emotions:** Our emotions are closely linked to our ability to hear spirits. By getting in touch with your feelings, you can start to become more attuned to the messages coming through.

- **Visualize What You Want to Hear:** If you are looking for guidance from your Spirit Guides, try to visualize what you would like to hear. This can help to open up the channel of communication.

Clairsentience
(What to Expect When You're Clairsentient)

Being clairsentient means that you experience psychic impressions through your feelings. In other words, you "know" things on a gut level, even if you can't explain how you know them. Clairsentience is one of the most common forms of psychic ability and is also one of the easiest to develop. As you open yourself up to your psychic abilities, you may find that your gut feelings become stronger and more accurate. With practice, you can learn to use your clairsentience to guide you in all areas of your life.

Clairsentience in Everyday Life

Clairsentient individuals often report having empathic abilities, meaning they can sense the emotions of others. They may also experience strong intuitions or "gut feelings" about people and situations. In addition, clairsentients often notice significant coincidences, or what is known as "synchronicity." While some people may dismiss these experiences as mere coincidence, clairsentients know they are receiving guidance from a higher source. They can navigate the world more intuitively by attuning to their inner feelings.

How to Develop Clairsentience

Most people are familiar with the five senses, but did you know that there is a sixth sense? This sense, known as clairsentience, refers to the ability to receive information from beyond the physical world. While some people are born with this ability, it is also possible to develop clairsentience through spiritual practice. Here are three ways to get started:

Connecting with Your Emotions: Clairsentience is often described as an "empathic" ability, meaning that those who can access this sense are very in tune with their emotions. If you want to develop your clairsentience, start by spending time getting in touch with your feelings. Notice what makes you feel good and what makes you feel bad. Pay attention to your intuition, and don't be afraid to trust your gut feeling.

Learning How to Meditate: Meditation is an excellent way to quiet the mind and focus on the present moment. When you meditate, you create a space for stillness and clarity. As you become more comfortable with meditation, you may start to notice intuitive insights emerging from the silence. These insights can be a valuable form of guidance from the Higher Self or Spirit Guides.

Practicing Grounding and Centering: To receive psychic information, it is important to be grounded and centered. This means that you are present in your body and aware of your surroundings. You can ground yourself by visualizing roots growing from your feet and anchoring you into the earth. To center yourself, focus on your breath, and let go of any thoughts or distractions. With practice, you'll become better at receiving clear and accurate information from the spiritual realm.

Tips for Improving Clairsentience

If you're interested in developing your clairsentience, there are a few things you can do to help the process along:

- **Commit to Exploring Your Psychic Ability Regularly:** The more you work with your clairsentience, the stronger it will become. To see results, it is important to be consistent with your practice. Set aside some time each day to focus on developing your psychic ability.

- **Be Open to All Forms of Communication:** Clairsentience is often described as a gut feeling, but it can also manifest in other ways. You may receive information through dreams, symbols, or even physical sensations. Pay attention to how you receive information and be open to all forms of communication from the spiritual realm.

- **Practice Discerning between Your Thoughts and Psychic Information:** It can be tricky to distinguish between your thoughts and psychic impressions. A good way to tell the difference is to ask yourself if the information you are receiving is based on fear or love. If the answer is fear, the information is likely coming from your mind. However, if the answer is love, it is more likely that the information is coming from a higher source.

- **Let Go of Expectations:** When you are first starting, it is important to let go of any expectations you have about the process. Psychic ability is a subtle sense, and it may take some time to get in touch with your clairsentient abilities. Be patient and trust that the information you need will be revealed in due time.

Claircognizance
(What to Expect When You're Claircognizant)

Claircognizance is a type of extrasensory perception that refers to the ability to know things without prior knowledge or understanding. This ability is often described as a "sixth sense" or "gut feeling," and it can be used to obtain information about people, places, events, or objects. Claircognizance differs from other forms of ESP, such as clairvoyance and clairaudience, in that it does not involve seeing or hearing things that are not ordinarily available to the senses. Instead, claircognizant individuals simply know things that they could not possibly know through normal means.

This form of extrasensory perception allows access to information unavailable through the five senses. It's also known as "clear knowing" or "inner knowing." Claircognizance often manifests as a strong inner knowing or hunch about something. It's a sense that goes beyond what you can see, hear, taste, smell, or touch. Although there is no scientific evidence to support the existence of Claircognizance, many people believe that this ability is real and that it can be harnessed to obtain valuable information.

Claircognizance in Everyday Life

Claircognizance can be used in various ways in everyday life. For example, you might receive divine guidance through Claircognizance. You might also use your intuition to make decisions based on your inner knowledge. Claircognizant people often become successful business owners, stockbrokers, and police officers because they know how to listen to their gut feelings and follow their instincts.

Claircognizance often manifests as a "gut feeling" about someone or something. You just know that something is true, even though there's no logical reason to feel that way. Claircognizance can be a very useful tool in everyday life. For example, you might use it to:

- **Make Decisions:** If you're trying to decide whether or not to take a new job, for example, you may get a claircognizant sense of whether or not it's the right choice for you.

- **Get Guidance:** Many people like to ask their claircognizant selves for advice on important decisions. All you need to do is focus on your question and then let the answer come to you.

- **Sense Danger:** If you're walking down a dark alley and suddenly get a strong sense that you're in danger, your Claircognizance is trying to warn you. Listen to your intuition and get out of there!

Claircognizance is just one of many different psychic abilities. Still, it's one that we can all use in our everyday lives if we learn how to listen to our intuition.

How to Develop Claircognizance

If you're interested in developing your claircognizant abilities, there are several things you can do to nurture this process. Meditation is one way to calm the mind and open yourself up to receiving inner guidance. You can also practice visualization exercises and ask for signs from the universe about a particular decision you're trying to make. Pay attention to your dreams, as they can also provide helpful guidance. As you begin to trust your inner knowing, you'll start to notice Claircognizance becoming a more regular part of your life. Claircognizance is a powerful gift that can help you live a more intuitive and fulfilling life.

Tips for Improving Claircognizance

If you want to improve your Claircognizance, there are a few things you can do:

- **Be Willing to Receive:** For Claircognizance to work, you must be willing to receive information from your higher self. If you're not open to the idea of inner guidance, you'll likely block any information that comes through.

- **Get Comfortable with Silence:** One of the best ways to open yourself up to claircognizant abilities is to get comfortable with silence. Meditation and mindfulness are excellent ways to quieten the mind and connect with your inner knowing.

- **Trust Your Intuition:** When you receive a hunch or feeling about something, trust it. The more you trust your intuition, the stronger your claircognizant abilities will become.

- **Be Patient:** Claircognizance is a process that takes time and patience. Don't expect to become an expert overnight. Trust that the information will come when you're ready to receive it.

- **Listen to Your Inner Voice:** We all have an inner voice that speaks to us. This is the voice of our higher selves. Pay attention to your inner voice and trust that it is guiding you in the right direction.

- **Follow Your Heart:** Our hearts are often wiser than our minds. If you're struggling to make a decision, follow your heart. It will usually lead you in the right direction.

The four main clairs are:

- Clairvoyance (seeing images),
- Clairaudience (hearing sounds),
- Clairsentience (recognizing feelings)
- Claircognizance (knowing).

We all have one or more of these skills, but they might be dormant, and we need to tap into them. In mediumship, clairvoyance is seeing images of the deceased or other beings in the spirit world. Clairaudience is hearing sounds, such as the voice of the deceased or other beings in the spirit world. Clairsentience recognizes feelings, such as the emotions of the deceased or other beings in the spirit world. Claircognizance knows things without having any physical evidence or logical explanation for why you do.

You can do several things to develop your Clair abilities, such as meditating, practicing visualization exercises, and asking for signs from the universe. You can also improve your clairs by getting comfortable with silence, trusting your intuition, and being patient. Remember to listen to your inner voice and follow your heart. The more you trust these abilities, the more they will become a part of your everyday life.

Chapter 6: Spirit Channeling 101

Have you ever wanted to connect with a loved one who has passed away? Or perhaps you're curious about your roots and want to connect with your ancestors? If so, you may be interested in learning about spirit channeling. Spirit channeling is a practice that allows you to connect with the spirits of deceased loved ones or ancestors. It's similar to mediumship, but there are some key differences. In this chapter, we'll explore what spirit channeling is, how it's different from mediumship, and how to do it.

Many different techniques can be used to channel spirits, but one of the most crucial things is to create a space where you feel safe.

Spirit Channeling

Many people are fascinated by the idea of spirit channeling, where a person becomes a medium for communicating messages from beyond the physical world. While some people may be skeptical of this practice, there is no doubt that it has been practiced for centuries in cultures worldwide. The ancient Egyptians, for example, believed that their Pharaohs were channels to the gods, and many indigenous peoples believed their shamans could communicate with spirits.

Some people believe that anyone can learn to channel spirits. In contrast, others believe it is a gift only certain people possess. Many different techniques can be used to channel spirits, but one of the most crucial things is to create a space where you feel safe and comfortable. This may mean lighting candles or incense or playing soothing music. Once you have created your space, you can begin to clear your mind and focus on your breath. It may take some time to reach a state of deep relaxation, but once you do, you may find that you can channel messages from beyond the physical world.

Mediumship vs. Spirit Channeling

When it comes to connecting with the world beyond, there are two main approaches that people take: mediumship and spirit channeling. Both of these practices can be used to communicate with spirits, but there are some key distinctions between them.

Although "mediumship" and "spirit channeling" are often used interchangeably, they refer to two different things. Mediumship is the ability to communicate with spirits who have passed on to the other side, while spirit channeling is the act of allowing a spirit to temporarily possess your body to communicate with the living. Channeling generally implies that the medium is not in control of the situation and that they are simply providing a vessel for the spirit to use.

Mediumship can be used for a variety of purposes, such as providing comfort to the bereaved or delivering messages from beyond the grave. Spirit channeling, on the other hand, is often used to gain insights or knowledge that would otherwise be unavailable. Channeled messages can come from various sources, including departed loved ones, guardian angels, or even higher beings such as Jesus or Buddha. Ultimately, whether you're seeking comfort or wisdom, both mediumship and spirit channeling can provide valuable insights into the afterlife.

Both mediumship and spirit channeling can provide information and guidance from the other side. However, each approach has its benefits and drawbacks. Mediumship may be more effective for communicating specific messages, while channeling may be better for receiving general information. Ultimately, it is up to the individual to decide which approach is best for them.

Spirit Channeling in Shamanism

Shamanism is an ancient spiritual practice involving communing with the spirit to heal the physical world. Central to shamanism is the belief that everything in the universe is connected and that disease or disharmony occurs when this connection is broken. Shamans enter into trances to journey to the spirit realm and repair these broken connections. This practice is known as "spirit channeling."

To journey to the spirit realm, shamans use various methods, such as drumming, dancing, singing, and visualization. Once they have entered into a trance state, they will often receive guidance from helpful spirits through symbols or images. By interpreting these messages, shamans can identify the root cause of a problem and take steps to correct it. In this way, spirit channeling can be a powerful tool for healing physical ills and restoring balance to the natural world.

Spirit Channeling in Voodoo

Voodoo is an Afro-Caribbean religious tradition that combines elements of West African Vodun, Catholicism, and Native American traditions. One of the most unique aspects of Voodoo is spirit channeling. This is a practice where a medium goes into a trance and allows a spirit to take over their body to communicate with the living.

Spirit channeling is said to be a very powerful experience, both for the person who is channeling and for those who are witnessing it. The spirit being channeled is said to be able to impart wisdom and knowledge they have gained in the afterlife, and they can also offer guidance and advice. For the person doing the channeling, it can be a deeply moving experience that helps them connect with their spirituality.

If you are interested in experiencing spirit channeling, you should seek out a reputable Voodoo priest or priestess. They will help you prepare for the experience and create a safe space for you to journey into the spirit world.

Spirit Channeling in Spiritualism

Spirit channeling is a practice that has been used for centuries by many different cultures. The basic idea is that a spirit world exists beyond our physical world and can communicate with these spirits. There are many ways to channel spirits, but the most common method is through mediumship. This involves going into a trance-like state and allowing the spirit to take control of your body and voice to communicate with the living.

Spiritualism is a religion where people believe in the existence of a spirit world and the ability to communicate with those who have passed on. Many spiritualists believe that we can all learn from the wisdom of the spirits and that they can help us better navigate our lives. Spirit channeling is one of the main ways spiritualists connect with the spirit world and is an essential part of their belief system.

Many resources are available online and in libraries, if you are interested in learning more about spiritualism or spirit channeling. There are also many spiritualist churches around the world where you can meet other like-minded people and explore this fascinating belief system.

The Trance State

All of these traditions have one thing in common: the trance state. This is a natural state of consciousness that we all experience every day. It is the state between wakefulness and sleep and a very powerful state for spirit channeling. To channel spirits, you must first enter into a trance state.

There are many ways to induce a trance state, but the most common method is through meditation. Meditation is a practice that allows you to focus your mind and achieve a state of deep relaxation. Once you reach this state, your conscious mind will be quiet, and you'll be more open to receiving messages from the spirit world. There are many different types of meditation, so find a method that works for you. If you are new to meditation, many resources are available online and in libraries. Once you have learned how to meditate, you can begin to practice spirit channeling.

Another way to enter into a trance state is through hypnosis. Hypnosis is a state of deep relaxation induced by another person. The person hypnotizing you'll guide you into a trance state and help you focus your mind. Once in a trance, you'll be more open to receiving messages from the spirit world. This method is often used by mediums who are trying to channel spirits.

Whether Voodoo, Shamanism, or Spiritualism, channeling always starts with the practitioner going into a trance state. This could be done through meditation, hypnosis, or any other method that works for the individual. Entering this trance state is a necessary step in communicating with the beyond. After entering a trance, you'll be more open to receiving messages from the spirit world. These messages can come in the form of thoughts, feelings, or images. Remember that not all messages will make sense to you, but trust that the message is coming from a place of love and wisdom. Allow the message to guide you, and trust that it is for your highest good.

Channeling Your Ancestors

Maybe you have heard of people channeling their ancestors before, but what does that mean exactly? Channeling is when an individual goes into a trance-like state and becomes possessed by the spirit of another. This can happen spontaneously or through specific techniques, such as meditation or chanting.

Those who practice ancestor worship believe that our ancestors are around us, even after they have passed on. They can offer guidance and protection, and staying in communication with them is vital. Channeling is one way to do this.

You open yourself to their knowledge and wisdom when you channel your ancestors. You may receive messages about your personal life, or they may offer advice about important decisions you need to make. You may even find yourself speaking in a different language or with a different accent.

Ancestor worship is an ancient practice that is still practiced today in many cultures around the world. If you are interested in channeling your ancestors, here are a few things you can do to get started:

1. Investigating Your Lineage

Have you ever wondered about your ancestors? Who were they? Where did they come from? What were their lives like? If you have questions about your lineage, consider spirit channeling as a way to investigate your ancestry. It can help you communicate with the spirit world to gain information about a person's past. This information can provide insights into your family history and help you to connect with your ancestors on a deeper level.

If you're interested in exploring your lineage through spirit channeling, you should keep a few things in mind. First, finding a reputable medium with experience communicating with the departed is crucial. Second, be open to receiving whatever information comes through, even if it isn't what you expected or hoped for. And finally, trust your intuition. If something doesn't feel right, don't hesitate to ask follow-up questions or request clarification. By following these guidelines, you can ensure that your experience is both safe and insightful.

2. Going into a Trance State

Spirit channeling your ancestors can be a powerful experience. Entering into a trance state is a crucial step here. This can be done through meditation, breathing exercises, or even sleep. Once you're in a trance state, focus your intention on contacting your ancestors. You may want to say their names out loud or visualize them in your mind. Then, simply open yourself up to receive any messages they may have for you. Remember that not all messages will come through clearly. Sometimes, you may only receive snippets of information or vague impressions. However, with practice, you should be able to receive messages that are clearer and more concise.

3. Connecting with an Ancestor

When trying to connect with an ancestor, there are a few things you can do to prepare. First, create a peaceful and comfortable space where you won't be disturbed. You might want to light some candles or incense or play soothing music. Next, focus your attention on your breath and allow yourself to relax. Once you're feeling calm and centered, begin to visualize the ancestor or loved one you wish to connect with. As you do so, imagine a bright white light surrounding you and filling the room. Picture the light merging with your energy until you feel locked into place.

Now, simply ask the ancestor or loved one for guidance. Allow whatever comes into your mind to flow freely without judgment. If you don't receive an answer immediately, that's okay - just be patient and keep an open mind. You may find that Spirit Channeling your ancestors can provide valuable insights and guidance on your life journey.

4. Receiving Messages

Although our ancestors are no longer with us in physical form, they can still offer guidance and support from the spirit world. One way to connect with them is through a technique where you open yourself up to receive messages. It can be done alone or with the help of a medium. The key is to relax and allow the messages to come through. You may hear them as a voice in your head, or you may receive visual images or feelings. Trust your intuition and go with whatever comes up. Keep an open mind, and don't be afraid to ask questions. Remember, your ancestors want to help you and will only give you helpful information.

5. Interpreting Messages

Channeling is a broadly defined term that can refer to any type of communication with spirits. This includes communicating with deceased loved ones, guides, angels, and other non-physical beings. Channeling can take many different forms, from hearing voices in your head to seeing visions in your mind's eye. However, the most important thing is to be open to receiving messages from the other side. Once you've established a connection, it's crucial to interpret the meaning of the message you've received. This can often be done using intuition or consulting with a trusted psychic or medium. With a little practice, you'll be surprised at how easy it is to channel your ancestors and receive guidance from the other side.

6. Coming out of the Trance State

After you've finished channeling your ancestors, it's very important that you carefully and slowly come out of the trance state. To do this, begin by focusing and taking a few deep breaths. Then, open your eyes and take a look around the room. Take a few moments to stretch and move your body before getting up and resuming your day. Remember that channeling can be a very powerful experience, so take some time to ground yourself afterward. By following these simple steps, you can ensure that you have a safe and successful experience channeling your ancestors.

7. Practice

If you're interested in spirit channeling, you may be wondering how to get started. After all, it's not something that you can just pick up overnight. However, the good news is that practice does make perfect. Many people are interested in channeling their ancestors but don't know how to go about it. The first step is to enter into a trance state. This can be done through meditation, prayer, or simply focusing your attention on your breath.

Once you have entered the trance state, relax and allow the energy of your ancestors to flow through you. You may feel them speaking to you or simply receive impressions and images. Trust whatever comes through, and do not try to force the experience. If you do feel called to speak aloud, do so respectfully and lovingly. Remember that your ancestors are here to help and guide you; they will do so in whatever way they feel is best.

Spirit Channeling Tips

If you've ever felt called to connect with the other side, you may wonder how to start channeling spirits. Here are some steps to help you:

1. Find a quiet place where you feel comfortable and relaxed. This will be your space for channeling, so make sure it's a place where you won't be interrupted.

2. Sit or recline in a comfortable position. You may want to close your eyes to help focus your attention inward.

3. Take several deep breaths and focus on letting go of any distractions or worries. Try to clear your mind and simply be present in the moment.

4. Once you feel centered and calm, focus your attention on your breath. Breathe deeply and slowly, and imagine each breath opening up your energy channels.

5. Visualize a white light emanating from your heart, filling your entire body with its peaceful, cleansing energy.

6. Now, invite the spirits you wish to communicate with to enter your light-filled space. Imagine them joining you in this safe and sacred space.

7. Ask the spirits any questions, and open yourself up to receive messages from them. You may hear them clearly in your mind, or they may come through as more subtle impressions or feelings. Trust whatever form the communication takes.

8. Thank the spirits for their time and guidance, and then visualize the white light again, this time expanding outward to engulf the space around you and drive away any negative

energies that may have attached themselves to you during the channeling session.

9. When you're ready, slowly open your eyes and take a few minutes to journal about your experience. Write down anything that stands out to you, no matter how small it may seem. Review these tips regularly until they become second nature! The more you practice, the easier it will be to channel spirits effectively—and safely!

Spirit channeling is a powerful way to connect with the other side and receive guidance from your ancestors. Mediumship and spirit channeling are different in that mediumship is passing on messages from the beyond, while spirit channeling is communicating directly with spirits. Shamanism, voodoo, and spiritualism are all different traditions that perceive and practice spirit channeling in different ways—but they all share the commonality of the trance state.

To channel spirits, you must first create a sacred space for yourself. This can be anywhere in your home where you feel comfortable and relaxed. Make sure to remove any distractions from this space, such as phones or television. You may also want to light some candles or incense to help set the mood. Once you're in your sacred space, take a few deep breaths and focus on your intention. Visualize your ancestors coming to you and ask them for guidance. Then, simply allow yourself to open up and receive whatever messages they have for you.

Remember, there's no right or wrong way to do this. Just go with the flow and trust that whatever comes through is meant for you. With a little practice, you'll be well on your way to channeling your ancestors!

Chapter 7: Channel Your Spirit Guides

As we journey through life, it can often feel like we are alone in the world. However, there is no need to feel like that, as we all have spirit guides who are there to help us. Spirit guides are powerful helpers who are always with us, even though we may not be aware of their presence. They can assist us in many ways, such as helping us with finding our purpose in life, providing comfort in times of difficulty, and guiding us when we need it most.

Many people believe in the existence of spirit guides.
https://www.pexels.com/photo/person-in-green-long-sleeve-shirt-sitting-on-brown-chair-7182627/

When we open ourselves up to the help of our spirit guides, we can live more fulfilling and joyful lives. This chapter will teach you about the different types of spirit guides that are available to help you on your journey. You'll also learn about some simple visualization exercises that can help you to connect with them. Finally, you'll be given tips on channeling your spirit guides so that you can receive their guidance more easily.

Spirit Guides

Many believe in spirit guides – unseen beings offering wisdom, guidance, and support. While some believe that we are each assigned a single spirit guide, others believe that we can have multiple guides – depending on our needs. Some say their guides come to them in dreams or meditation, while others claim to have never seen or heard their guides.

A spirit guide is an entity that is here to help us on our journey through life. They are often referred to as our guardian angels but can take many different forms. Spirit guides can be animals, plants, or even inanimate objects. They can also be deceased loved ones, such as a grandparent or close friend. It is believed that we each have at least one spirit guide, but we may have many more.

Whether or not you believe in the existence of spirit guides, there's no denying that they make for interesting stories. Guides are often said to be wise and all-knowing and are usually used as a force for good. Suppose you're ever feeling lost or confused. In that case, it might be worth considering the possibility that you have a spirit guide who is trying to help you find your way.

Types of Spirit Guides

There are many different types of spirit guides, each with a unique role to play in our lives. Some guides can help us to find our purpose, those who offer comfort and support, and those who give us practical advice. Whatever their form, spirit guides can offer us guidance, support, and protection when we need it most. Here are some of the most common types of spirit guides:

1. Angels

Angels are beings of light and love and are often called upon to provide guidance and support during difficult times. They can also help us connect with our higher selves and true purpose in life. While we all have guardian angels who watch over us, we can also choose to work with other angels who can offer specific types of support and guidance. If you feel called to work with an angel, there are many ways to go about it. You can meditate on their energy, ask for their help during prayer or visualization, or even keep a picture of them nearby as a reminder of their presence. However you choose to connect with them, know they are always here to support and guide you on your journey.

2. Spirit Animals

Many cultures believe that each person has a spirit animal, which is a reflection of their inner self. The idea of a spirit animal is thought to have originated with the shamans of ancient times, who would communicate with animals to gain wisdom and understanding. Many modern-day cultures have adopted this concept, which is now seen as a way to connect with nature and the animal kingdom. People often choose their spirit animal based on qualities they admire or identify with. For example, someone who is courageous might choose a lion as their spirit animal, while someone wise might choose an owl. By connecting with their spirit animal, people hope to gain some of the positive qualities that the animal possesses.

3. Plant Allies

In many cultures, plants are seen as powerful allies and teachers. For centuries, indigenous peoples have relied on plant medicine for physical and spiritual healing. Today, working with plant spirits is known as "plant ally work."

Plant ally work can take many forms. Some people work with plant spirits for guidance and wisdom, while others use plant medicine for healing. Some people even choose to live in close relationships with plants, spending time in nature and learning from the ones around them.

There are many ways to connect with plant spirits. One common practice is to spend time in nature and simply open yourself up to receiving guidance from the plants. You can also try asking specific questions and then listening for the answer in your heart. Many people find it helpful to keep a journal to record their experiences and insights.

If you're interested in working with plant spirits, many resources are available to help you get started. Books, websites, and even online courses can introduce you to the basics of plant ally work. You may also want to seek out a local teacher or shaman who can guide you on your journey. Remember that the most crucial thing is to follow your heart and trust your intuition.

4. Deceased Loved Ones

Many believe that we are all accompanied by spirit guides throughout our lives. These guides can take many different forms, but one of the most common is that of a deceased loved one. It is thought that our loved ones choose to stay with us after death to help us through difficult times and offer guidance when needed. Some people say that they have received guidance from a deceased loved one in dreams or visions, while others claim to have heard their voice during meditation or moments of clarity. While there is no scientific proof of the existence of spirit guides, the belief provides comfort and hope for many people. Whether or not you believe in spirit guides, it is clear that the idea of having a deceased loved one watch over you can be a source of great comfort.

5. Ascended Masters

The Ascended Masters are one of the most well-known types of spirit guides. These are beings who have reached a high level of spiritual development and now serve as mentors and teachers for those still on our spiritual journey. They can take on many different forms and often appear to us in our dreams or meditation. They are here to help us learn, grow, and develop our spiritual gifts. If you feel called to work with an Ascended Master, know that a powerful force is guiding you for good. Trust your intuition and follow your heart. You are being led in the right direction.

Visualization Exercises

If you're looking to connect with your spirit guide, one of the best things you can do is simply close your eyes and visualize. Picture your guide in whatever form they take – human, animal, or even a ball of light. See them standing or floating next to you, and imagine yourself reaching out to touch them. As you focus on this image, see if any feelings or impressions come to mind. Do they have a message for you? Are they trying to show you something?

Just allow whatever comes to your flow freely, and don't try to force anything. Remember, the goal is simply to relax and open yourself up to receiving guidance from your spirit guide. With a little practice, you should be able to connect with them anytime, anywhere. Here are different ways you can work with your spirit guide, depending on what form they take:

1. Connecting with Your Angels

Imagine yourself in a beautiful meadow surrounded by friendly animals. The sun is shining, and the breeze is gentle. You feel safe and loved. You see two angelic beings standing next to you as you look around. They radiate love and light and are here to protect and support you. Listen to what they have to say. What do they tell you about your life Purpose? What do they offer guidance about? Thank them for their help, and then let them go.

Return to the present moment, and take some time to journal about your experience. How did it feel to connect with your angels? What wisdom did they share with you? Allow this visualization exercise to deepen your understanding of your relationship with the divine realm.

2. Connecting with Your Spirit Animal

Close your eyes and take a few deep breaths. Imagine yourself in a field of tall grass. The sun is shining, and the breeze is blowing. You see a path in front of you, and you begin to walk along this path. As you do, you notice a beautiful creature standing in the distance. It is your spirit animal. As you approach, the animal comes to meet you. It looks into your eyes and nuzzles your hand. You feel a sense of peace and connection with this creature. You spend some time together, and then the animal runs off into the distance. As you watch it go, you feel refreshed and uplifted. This is your spirit animal, and it is always with you, guiding and supporting you on your journey through life.

3. Connecting with a Deceased Loved One

It can be difficult to cope with the loss of a loved one. Even if we know that they are no longer suffering, it can be hard to let go. One way to facilitate the grieving process is through visualization exercises. Connecting with a deceased loved one through visualization can create a sense of closure and peace.

To begin, find a comfortable place to sit or lie down. Close your eyes and take a few deep breaths. Once you are feeling relaxed, picture your loved one in your mind's eye. They may appear as they did in life or come to you in a different form. Allow yourself to spend some time simply enjoying their company. Then, ask them any of the questions you have been carrying around since their death. You may want to ask about their experience of dying, what they see now, or what message they would like to share with you. Listen carefully to their answers, and trust that whatever they tell you is meant for you and will help you to heal. Finally, say goodbye and allow them to go. Thank them for coming to visit.

When you are finished, take a few minutes to journal about your experience. What did you see? What did your loved one tell you? How do you feel now? Allow yourself to process whatever comes up for you, knowing that each time you connect with your loved one in this way, it will become easier and more natural.

4. Connecting with Ascended Masters

As you close your eyes and begin to relax, take a few deep breaths and allow your mind to wander. Picture yourself in a beautiful garden, surrounded by blue sky and white clouds. In the center of the garden is a large tree, and sitting at the base of the tree is an Ascended Master. This being of light is benevolent and wise, and they are here to help you on your journey.

As you approach, the Ascended Master smiles and opens their arms to you. You feel a sense of peace and love as you embrace them. Then, ask the Ascended Master any question that is on your mind. Listen carefully to their answer, and trust that they are guiding you in the right direction. Thank them for their time, and then slowly open your eyes and return to the present moment. Take a few deep breaths, and know you are always connected to the Ascended Masters.

5. Connecting with a Plant Ally

Plants are living beings and are here to help us in our journey through life. When we connect with them in a spirit of love and respect, they can teach us many things. To connect with a plant ally, find a comfortable place to sit or lie down. Close your eyes and take a few deep breaths. Picture yourself in a beautiful meadow surrounded by wildflowers. In the distance, you see a tree that is calling you.

As you approach, you notice the tree glowing with a soft light. You reach out and place your hand on the tree trunk, and you feel a deep connection with this being. Ask the tree any question on your mind, and then listen carefully to the answer. Thank the tree for its time, and then slowly open your eyes and return to the present moment. Take a few deep breaths, and know that you are always connected to the plant kingdom.

How to Channel Your Spirit Guides

We all have spirit guides – those unseen helpers who offer guidance and support on our life journey. Unfortunately, many of us are not attuned to their presence and their wisdom. If you're seeking to connect with your guides, you can do a few things to channel their energy.

1. Meditation

Channeling your spirit guides can provide you with invaluable insights and guidance. One of the best ways to connect with your guides is through meditation. Before you begin, find a comfortable place to sit or lie down. Close your eyes and take a few deep breaths. Once you're feeling relaxed, start to focus on your breath. Slowly exhale and, as you do, visualize a white light emanating from your heart. This light will help to ground and protect you as you open yourself up to the energies of the Universe.

Next, imagine a golden cord connecting your heart to the infinite source of love and light. Take a few deep breaths and allow yourself to be filled with this divine energy. When you're ready, begin asking your guides for guidance or clarity on a specific issue. Be open to receiving whatever messages come through, whether it's in the form of images, words, or feelings. After you've finished meditating, take a few minutes to journal about your experience. Don't worry if you didn't receive any clear messages at first. It can sometimes take a bit of practice to channel your guides. With time and patience, you'll be able to connect with them whenever you need their guidance.

2. Automatic Writing

Channeling your spirit guides can be a great way to receive guidance and clarity on your life path. Another approach to communicating with your guides is automatic writing. It is a form of channeling where you allow the thoughts and words of your spirit guides to flow through you and onto the page. To practice automatic writing, find a quiet place where you won't be interrupted. Sit down with a pen and paper, and take a few deep breaths to relax your mind and body. Then, simply allow your hand to move across the paper, writing whatever words or thoughts come naturally from your hand.. Trust that whatever you write comes from a place of love and guidance, and be open to receiving whatever messages your guides have for you.

3. Psychometry

Psychometry is a psychic ability that allows people to receive information about an object or person by touching it. It is believed that everyone can use psychometry, but some people are more attuned to it than others. To try it for yourself, all you need is an object that belongs to the person you want to connect with. Once you have the object, hold it in your hands and focus on it. As you do so, try to clear your mind and open yourself up to any impressions or messages that come through. You may experience visions, hear voices, or simply get a sense of the person's energy. There is no right or wrong way to do this, so go with whatever feels most natural to you. With a little practice, you should be able to use psychometry to connect with your spirit guides and receive the guidance you seek.

4. Divination

Divination is a great way to start if you're curious about connecting with your spirit guides. Divination is the practice of using tools like tarot cards, crystal balls, or runes to gain insight into the future or to receive guidance from one's spirit guides. While some people view divination as a way to predict the future, it can also be used as a tool for self-exploration and growth. If you're interested in trying divination, there are many different techniques to choose from. Some popular methods include tarot reading, rune casting, and scrying. When choosing a method, it's important to go with what feels right for you. Trust your intuition and let your spirit guides guide you to the divination method that is best for you.

5. Dreaming

Dreams are a way for our subconscious mind to communicate with us, and they can be powerful tools for self-discovery. To channel your spirit guides through dreaming, start by keeping a dream journal. Write down your dreams as soon as you wake up, including as many details as possible. Then, start to notice any patterns that emerge. Are there certain symbols or messages that keep appearing? These may be signs from your spirit guides. Pay attention to your feelings and intuition when interpreting your dreams, as this is how your guides will communicate with you. With a little practice, you'll be able to channel your spirit guides through dreaming and receive the guidance you need.

Spirit guides are powerful allies that can offer guidance and support on your spiritual journey. It can be a guardian angel, a plant ally, an animal guide, or any other type of divine being that you feel a connection. If you're interested in connecting with your spirit guides, you can use many different techniques. Some popular methods include trance channeling, automatic writing, psychometry, divination, and dreaming. Trust your intuition and let your spirit guides guide you to the method that is best for you. Keep an open mind and trust whatever messages you receive. With a little practice, you'll be able to connect with your spirit guides and receive the guidance you seek.

Chapter 8: Cleansing and Protecting Yourself

As a medium, it's crucial to keep yourself and your environment clean. Regular cleansing removes any negativity you may have picked up from spiritual work and protects you from unwanted attachments. There are lots of different ways to cleanse yourself and your home, so choose the method that feels right for you. You may want to burn sage or palo santo, use crystals or smudge sticks, or simply take a salt bath. Remember that cleansing is an ongoing process, so regularly cleanse yourself and your space.

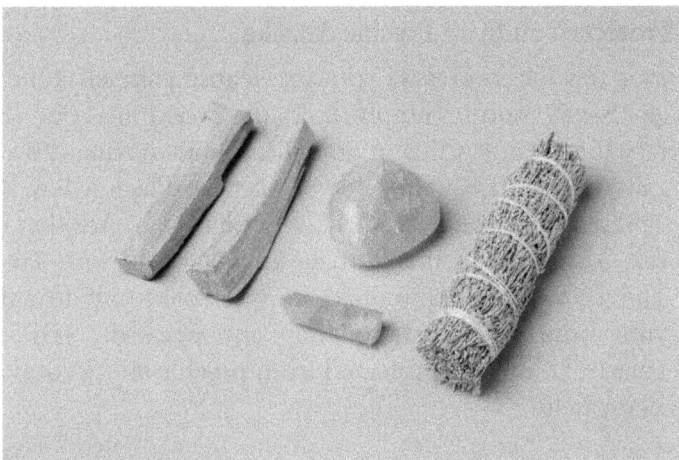

It's crucial to cleanse yourself before and after each seance or reading.
https://www.pexels.com/photo/photo-of-sage-beside-rose-quartz-4040591/

This chapter will teach you the importance of cleansing, different methods, and how to perform various cleansing rituals. You'll also learn about banishing rituals, which remove negative energy, curses, or entities from your home. By the end of this chapter, you'll be equipped with the knowledge you need to keep yourself and your environment safe and clean.

Importance of Cleansing

Cleansing is an essential part of being a medium. As you open yourself up to the spiritual world, you become more susceptible to picking up negative energy. This can lead to problems like psychic attacks, possession, and even depression. Cleansing yourself and your environment regularly helps to protect you from these negative energies and attachments. Cleaning yourself before and after each seance or reading is also crucial, as this will help remove any unwanted energies you may have picked up during the session.

1. Helps to Remove Negativity

Cleansing removes any unwanted energies that may have gotten attached to you and promotes balance and harmony within your energy field. There are several different ways to cleanse yourself, but one of the most effective is using crystals. Crystals can help to absorb and release negative energies, and they can also help to promote a sense of calm and well-being. If you want to cleanse yourself regularly, then using crystals is worth considering.

2. Protects You from Psychic Attacks

There are a few different ways you can cleanse yourself. One is to use sage or Palo Santo wood. Simply hold the wood in your hand and smudge yourself with it, starting at your head and moving down to your feet. You can also cleanse yourself with crystals. Place a few stones on your body and allow their energy to flow through you. Another option is to take a salt bath. Add some Himalayan salt or Epsom salt to your bathwater and relax for 20 minutes. As you soak, visualize the water cleansing your aura and washing away any negativity. By cleansing yourself regularly, you'll stay protected from psychic attacks and maintain a healthy energy field.

3. Reduces the Risk of Attachment

Mediumship can be a rewarding and life-changing experience, but it also comes with some inherent risks. One of the most common risks is attachment – when the spirit of a deceased individual begins to attach itself to the medium. This can be harmful to both parties, as it can prevent the medium from moving on and living their life. Cleansing is one way to reduce the risk of attachment, as it helps clear away any residual energy clinging to the medium. There are many different ways to cleanse, but some common methods include sage smudging, crystal cleansing, and sacred baths. Taking time to cleanse after each mediumship session can help reduce the risk of attachment and keep yourself healthy and balanced.

4. Can Help You to Develop Your Skills

Cleansing can clear away any negative energy that might be clinging to you, and it can also help to raise your vibration. This, in turn, can make it easier for you to connect with spirit Guides and loved ones who have passed on. When you're free from negative energy, you'll be able to focus more clearly on your mediumship skills and develop them more quickly. The more you practice, the better you'll become at connecting with the other side.

5. Protects from Possession and Depression

One of the most vital things you can do as a medium is cleansing yourself regularly. Not only will this remove any negative energy that you may have picked up, but it will also protect you from possession and help you stay grounded and connected to your guides. Some of the best ways to cleanse yourself include sage smudging, crystal cleansing, and salt baths. By cleaning regularly, you can help keep yourself safe and healthy and develop your mediumship skills more quickly.

Methods of Cleansing

While every medium will have their preferred method of cleansing, there are a few that are more commonly used. Here are some of the most popular ones:

1. Smudging

Smudging is a ceremonial way of cleansing and purifying a space or person with the smoke of specific dried herbs. Some of the most popular herbs for smudging include sage, sweetgrass, and cedar. When smudging, it is crucial to set your intention. For example, you may want to cleanse your space of negative energy or invite in positive energy. Once your intention is set, light the herb and allow it to smolder. Wash the smoke around your body or space using your hand or a feather. Start at the feet and move up to the head. As you do this, visualize the smoke taking away any negative energy. Once you have cleansed yourself or your space, extinguish the herb and thank it for its service.

2. Visualization

One method that can be especially effective for cleansing is visualization. This involves picturing yourself surrounded by white light or any other type of light you feel drawn to. As you picture the light surrounding you, visualize it cleansing your aura and washing away any negativity. You may also want to visualize the light entering your body and filling you with positive energy.

To visualize, simply close your eyes and picture a white light surrounding your body. This light will help to cleanse your energy field and remove any negative or unwanted energies. Visualize the light moving up and down your body, starting at your feet and moving up to your head. Take a few deep breaths and allow yourself to relax into the visualization. Once you feel that you have been fully cleansed, you can open your eyes and resume your work.

3. Reiki

Reiki is a method of natural healing that can be used to cleanse and balance the body's energy systems. It is based on the belief that an invisible life force energy surrounds the bodies. When this energy is in balance, we are healthy and well. Reiki works by channeling this life force energy into the body through the hands of a trained practitioner. This breaks up any blockages or imbalances in the flow of energy, allowing the body to heal itself. Reiki is a gentle and effective way to cleanse the body and promote healing, and it can be used on both people and animals. If you are interested in trying Reiki, many qualified practitioners would be happy to help you experience its benefits.

4. Crystals

As a medium, it is crucial to keep your energy field clean and free of negative attachments. There are many ways to do this, but cleansing crystals is one of the most effective. They can help to remove negative energy from your auric field, as well as help protect you from further psychic attacks. When selecting crystals for cleansing, choose those that resonate with your energy field. Some of the most popular crystals for cleansing include amethyst, black tourmaline, and selenite. These stones can be used in various ways, such as being placed on your body during meditation or worn as jewelry. In whichever way you choose to use them, incorporating cleansing crystals into your mediumship practice can help ensure that you operate from a place of purity and light.

5. Sound Healing

Sound healing is a method of cleansing for mediums that uses sound waves to cleanse and balance the energy in your space. This type of cleansing is said to be especially effective for removing negative energy and promoting physical and emotional healing. Sound healing can be used in a variety of ways, such as through the use of singing bowls, chimes, or gongs. It can also be done simply by listening to calming music or sounds.

To use sound healing for cleansing, simply find a comfortable place to sit or lie down. Close your eyes and begin to focus on your breath. As you breathe in and out, allow the sound of the music or instruments to wash over you. Visualize the sound waves entering your body and cleansing your aura. Continue to breathe deeply and focus on the sound until you feel that you have been fully cleansed.

Cleansing Rituals

As a medium, it is vital to regularly cleanse your energy field to maintain your psychic ability. Negativity can build up over time, and it is essential to release this energy regularly. There are many different ways to cleanse your energy, and you can choose the method or methods that work best for you. Some people prefer to do a full-body cleansing ritual daily, while others may only do it once a week or so. Listen to your body and intuition to determine what is best for you. Nevertheless, here are a few popular cleansing rituals that you may want to try:

1. Full Moon Cleanse

Full moon cleanses are a great way to release old energy and make space for new beginnings. A full moon cleansing ritual can be done alone or with a group of other mediums. To begin, sit or stand in a circle. If you are using candles, place them in the center of the circle. Take a few deep breaths and focus on your intention for the cleansing. Then, each person in the circle should say aloud one thing that they would like to release. This can be anything that is no longer serving you, such as a negative emotion or belief.

Once everyone has spoken, take a few minutes to meditate on what you are letting go of. When you are ready, start the cleansing by visualizing white light entering your body and pushing out any negativity. You can also use sage or palo santo to cleanse your energy field. Continue until you feel cleansed and balanced.

2. New Moon Cleanse

A new moon cleansing is similar to a full moon cleansing. Still, it focuses on setting future intentions rather than releasing old energy. This can be done in several ways, but some basic steps include: clearing your home of negative energy, setting intentions for the month ahead, and cleansing your body and mind. To clear your home, you can smudge with sage or palo santo, use an energy spray, or simply open all the doors and windows to let fresh air in.

Once your home is cleared, you can set your intentions by writing them down on a piece of paper or creating a vision board. Finally, cleanse your body and mind by taking a salt bath, drinking plenty of water, and meditating. Performing this ritual at the beginning of each month will help keep your energy clean and aligned with your highest self.

3. Solar Eclipse Cleanse

A solar eclipse is an ideal time to cleanse your energy field, as the increased energies can help release any heaviness or negativity you may be carrying. There are many different ways to perform a solar eclipse cleanse. One simple method is to take a saltwater bath using either Epsom salts or sea salt. You can also add a few drops of lavender oil to help promote relaxation and peace.

As you take your bath, imagine the water washing away any unwanted energies, leaving you feeling refreshed and rejuvenated. When you're done, make sure to drink plenty of water to help flush any toxins from your system. Regular cleansing rituals like this can help ensure that your energy field is clear and free-flowing.

4. Lunar Eclipse Cleanse

A lunar eclipse is another powerful time to cleanse your energy field. This can be done similarly to a solar eclipse cleansing – but with a few tweaks to suit the moon's energies. For example, you may want to add some lunar-associated herbs to your baths, such as jasmine or chamomile. You can also add a few drops of moonstone oil to your bathwater. This stone is particularly helpful in releasing emotions and past traumas. As with a solar eclipse, imagine the water washing away any negative energy, leaving you feeling lighter and brighter. When you've finished, make sure you drink plenty of water to help flush any toxins from your system.

5. Equinox Cleanse

As the seasons change, it can be a good time to cleanse your body, mind, and spirit. One way to do this is through a cleansing ritual. There are many different types of cleansing rituals, but one that is particularly well-suited for mediums is an Equinox Cleanse. This type of cleansing helps to realign your energy with the changing energies of the Earth. To perform this, you'll need a bowl of salt water, a white candle, and a piece of quartz crystal.

Begin by lighting the candle and placing it in front of you. Then, hold the quartz crystal in your left hand and dip it into the salt water. As you do this, visualize your life's negativity being washed away. Next, take a deep breath and release it slowly. Repeat this process three times. Finally, blow out the candle and allow the quartz crystal to air dry. As you perform this cleansing ritual, you should feel your energy shifting and aligning with the Earth's natural rhythms.

6. Solstice Cleanse

December is a month full of holidays and celebrations. For many people, it is a time to reflect on the past year and set their intention for the year to come. It is also a time when the veil between the spiritual and physical worlds is at its thinnest. As a result, December is an ideal time for mediums to perform a cleansing ritual. The solstice cleanse is a simple but powerful ritual that can help to clear away any unwanted energy and prepare you for the year ahead.

To begin, light a white candle and say: "I release all that no longer serves me. I welcome only that which is for my highest good." Then, take a few deep breaths and imagine yourself surrounded by white light. Visualize the light cleansing your aura of any negative energy. Next, hold each of your crystals in the candle flame for a few seconds, saying: "I cleanse you of all negativity." Finally, bury your crystals in the earth overnight, releasing any remaining unwanted energy. By performing this cleansing ritual, you'll help to create a space for positive energy to flow into your life.

Banishment Rituals

Banishment rituals are a necessary part of being a medium. As a medium, you are constantly surrounded by good and bad spirits. It is essential to keep the bad spirits away so they do not influence your work or harm those around you. There are many different banishment rituals that you can use, but the most crucial thing is that you are comfortable with the ritual and that it works for you. Some people prefer to use salt or holy water, while others use more elaborate rituals involving candles and incantations. Ultimately, the choice is up to you. Just remember that banishing rituals are vital to being a responsible medium.

1. Banishing Ritual for Negative Energy

There are certain banishing rituals that you can do to cleanse your space and get rid of any unwanted energy. One simple but effective method is to smudge your home with sage. This will help to clear the air and create a more positive vibration. You can also try using crystals such as selenite or black tourmaline to absorb negative energy. If you find yourself regularly surrounded by negative influences, it may be time to take a break from mediumship and focus on raising your vibration. By doing this, you'll be better equipped to handle any negativity that comes your way.

2. Banishing Ritual for a Curse or Hex

Suppose you suspect that you or someone you know has been cursed or hexed by a malicious spirit. In that case, you can take steps to banish the negative energy and protect yourself from further harm. First, understand that curses and hexes are a very real part of the spiritual world and should not be taken lightly. If you think you may have been cursed, you should first seek help from a medium or psychic who can assess the situation and identify the source of the curse.

Once the source has been identified, the medium will then work with you to perform a banishing ritual. This usually involves cleansing the area with sage smoke or holy water and then using powerful visualization techniques to force the negative energy out. With the help of a skilled medium, banishing curses and hexes is relatively straightforward - but it's always best to be cautious and take precautions to protect yourself from these dark forces.

3. Banishing Ritual for Ghosts, Spirits, and Entities

Suppose you are regularly dealing with ghosts, spirits, or entities. In that case, it is critical to have a reliable banishing ritual that you can use to send them away. This ritual should be performed whenever you feel like you are being followed or watched by an unwanted presence. To begin, light a white candle and say: "I banish you from this space. You are not welcome here." Then, use your fingers to trace a circle around the candle three times clockwise. As you do this, visualize a protective barrier forming around you. Finally, blow out the candle and say: "I release you from this space. You are free to go." This banishing ritual will clear your space and protect you from any unwanted entities.

Cleansing and banishing rituals are a necessary part of being a medium. These rituals will also create a more positive vibration in your space, benefiting you and those around you. This chapter provided an overview of some basic cleansing and banishing rituals that you can use to protect yourself. Remember, the most crucial thing is to find a method that works for you and that you feel comfortable with. With the help of these cleansing and banishing rituals, you can keep yourself safe and protected from any negative influences.

Chapter 9: The Power of Scrying

Scrying is an ancient practice that has been used for centuries to gain insight and knowledge. It has been used for everything from divination and fortune-telling to communicating with spirits and gaining spiritual guidance. While the exact origins of scrying are unknown, it is thought to date back to at least the early Egyptians, who used polished obsidian mirrors for scrying.

Scrying is an ancient practice that has been used for centuries to gain insight and knowledge.
https://www.pexels.com/photo/crop-soothsayer-predicting-fate-with-magic-ball-at-home-4790577/

Today, many people worldwide still practice scrying, who believe in its power to offer insights and knowledge that can be difficult to obtain through other means. Whether looking for answers to life's big questions or simply seeking guidance from your higher self, scrying may be worth a try. This chapter will teach you everything you need to know about scrying, from the different types to how to interpret your visions.

Scrying Defined

Scrying is a practice that has been used for centuries for divination and fortune-telling. The word "scrying" comes from the Old English word "descry," which means "to reveal." Scrying is typically done by gazing into a crystal ball, a mirror, a bowl of water, or any other reflective surface. As you gaze at the surface, you may see images appear before your eyes. These images can be interpreted in many ways, depending on the person doing the scrying.

Some people believe that images are premonitions of future events, while others believe that they are symbols that must be interpreted. Scrying is a deeply personal practice, and there is no right or wrong way to do it. Whether you use a traditional method like crystal ball gazing or something more unique like tea leaf reading, the important thing is to relax and let your mind be open to whatever messages may come through.

There are many different ways to scry, and each person may have their preferences. Some common methods include using a crystal ball, a pool of water, a mirror, or a flame. When scrying, it is important to enter into a relaxed state of mind to allow messages from the other side to come through. Once you have entered into a meditative state, you can begin to focus on your question or intent. The answer may come in the form of symbols, images, or words. Scrying can be an effective way to receive guidance from the other side and connect with your intuition. With practice, anyone can learn how to scry.

Crystal Ball Scrying

Scrying is an ancient art that involves gazing into a reflective surface to induce a trance-like state. Crystal balls have been used for scrying since at least the 16th century and are still popular among modern-day practitioners. There are a few different ways to use a crystal ball for scrying. One method is simply gazing into the ball and allowing your mind to wander. Another way is to ask a question and then wait for an image or symbol to appear in the ball. Some people also like to light candles or incense and create a relaxing atmosphere before scrying.

Whatever method you choose, remember that the most important thing is to relax and let your intuition guide you.

Pros and Cons

Scrying is one of the oldest and most popular forms of divination, with roots in ancient cultures such as Egypt, Greece, and China. The method can be used for navigation purposes, finding lost objects, or even communicating with spirits. While many people believe that scrying is a powerful tool for gaining insight into the future, there are also some drawbacks to this form of divination. One downside is that it can be difficult to interpret the images that are seen in the crystal ball. This means that scrying can sometimes be more frustrating than helpful. Additionally, because scrying requires a great deal of concentration, it can be taxing on both the body and mind. For these reasons, weighing the pros and cons of scrying is important before deciding whether to try it.

Step-By-Step Instructions

If you've never tried scrying before, it can seem like a daunting task. However, with a little practice, anyone can learn.

1. Find a quiet, comfortable place where you won't be interrupted. Make sure the area is well-lit so you can see the crystal ball.

2. Sit in a comfortable position and hold the crystal ball in your hands. Close your eyes and take a few deep breaths.

3. When ready, open your eyes and gaze into the crystal ball. Allow your mind to wander and see what images appear.

4. If you have a question you would like answered, focus on that question as you gaze into the ball.

5. Once you're finished scrying, reflect on what you saw for a few moments. Write down any impressions or images you saw in a journal for future reference.

Fire Scrying

Fire Scrying is a technique that has been used for centuries as a way of divination and fortune-telling. Fire scrying uses fire as a focal point. The act of scrying involves staring into a fire to induce a trance-like state, during which visions and messages may be received. It can be an effective way to receive guidance from your higher self or spirit guides. It is a simple yet powerful method for tapping into your intuition and accessing hidden knowledge. Give it a try the next time you need some clarity or guidance.

Pros and Cons

Many people find fire scrying to be an effective way of gaining clarity and insights into their lives. Still, there are also some potential drawbacks to this practice. One downside of fire scrying is that it can be very hard on the eyes, and it is crucial to take breaks frequently to avoid eye strain. Additionally, some people find the flickering flames to be distracting or even unsettling. Finally, because fire scrying requires such intense focus, it is important to be in a quiet and safe place where you will not be interrupted. Despite these potential drawbacks, this type can be a powerful tool for those who know how to use it effectively.

Step-By-Step Instructions

If you've never tried fire scrying, here are some simple instructions to get you started.

1. Find a quiet, safe place where you can build a small fire. You'll also need a metal bowl or cauldron to place the fire in.

2. Once you have everything you need, build a small fire in the bowl or cauldron. Allow the flames to burn for a few minutes until they become steady.

3. Sit in front of the fire and gaze into the flames. Relax your mind and body, and let your thoughts flow freely.

4. After a few minutes, you may begin to see images or receive messages in the form of mental impressions. Write down any insights that you receive in a journal for future reference.

Water Scrying

Water scrying is an ancient practice. Also known as crystal gazing, water scrying involves staring into a bowl of water to reveal hidden messages or visions. While the practice may sound simple, it requires focus and concentration to work. Many people believe that water scrying is a powerful tool for divination, and it has been used for centuries to help people make important decisions. If you're interested in trying water scrying, all you need is a bowl of clean water and a quiet place to focus. You may not see anything right away, but with patience and practice, you may be surprised by what you can see.

Pros and Cons

Water scrying is a form of divination that involves gazing into a bowl of water to gain insight into the future. Some people believe that water scrying is more accurate than other forms of divination because water is a natural element that is connected to all life. Others argue that water scrying is no more accurate than any other form of fortune-telling. While no scientific evidence supports either claim, water scrying can be a fun and interesting way to gain insights into the future.

Water scrying can be an enjoyable way to pass the time and gain some insight into the future. However, remember that it should not be taken too seriously. Like all forms of fortune-telling, it should be considered entertainment rather than a source of true information about the future.

Step-By-Step Instructions

Several different techniques can be used for water scrying. If you're interested in trying water scrying, you need a bowl of clean water and a quiet place to focus.

1. Fill a bowl with clean water and set it in front of you. You may want to add a drop of food coloring to the water to make it easier to see.

2. Sit in front of the bowl and stare into the water. Relax your mind and body, and let your thoughts flow freely.

3. After a few minutes, you may begin to see images or receive messages in the form of mental impressions. Write down any insights that you receive in a journal for future reference.

Mirror Scrying

Mirror scrying is a type of divination that involves gazing into a reflective surface to gain information about the future. Although any type of mirror can be used for scrying, many people prefer to use black mirrors, as they believe they can better capture and reflect energy. When practicing, you may see images appear on the mirror's surface. These images can symbolize anything from future events to messages from your subconscious mind. With practice, you'll learn to interpret these images and use them to gain insights into your life.

Pros and Cons

While there are many potential benefits to this practice, there are also some drawbacks that should be considered. One of the main advantages of mirror scrying is that it can be done with very little equipment. All you need is a mirror and a quiet place to focus your attention. This makes it an ideal divination method for people who are just starting or who don't have access to more specialized tools. Additionally, it can be used for various purposes, from gaining self-knowledge to peering into other people's lives. However, there are also some disadvantages to consider.

One potential downside is that staring into a mirror for extended periods can be taxing on the eyes. It's important to take breaks and rest your eyes if you start to feel discomfort. Additionally, some people find that they become too focused on their reflection during mirror scrying sessions, which can prevent them from seeing the greater picture. If you find yourself getting too caught up in your image, it might be helpful to try using a black or dark-colored cloth to cover the mirror until you're ready to end your session.

Overall, mirror scrying is a versatile and effective form of divination that can yield valuable insights. However, as with any type of divination, it's important to approach it with caution and an open mind.

Step-By-Step Instructions

If you're interested in trying mirror scrying for yourself, all you need is a mirror and a quiet place to focus. To get started, follow these simple steps:

1. Find a mirror that's large enough for you to comfortably gaze into. A black mirror is often used for this purpose, but any type of mirror will work.

2. Place the mirror in front of you and sit down. Relax your mind and body, and let your thoughts flow freely.

3. After a few minutes, you may see images appear on the mirror's surface. These images can symbolize anything from future events to messages from your subconscious mind. Write down any insights you receive in a journal for future reference.

Ink Scrying

Ink scrying is a form of divination that involves looking at patterns in ink, coffee, or tea stains. As you look at the ink, you may start to see shapes and patterns forming. These shapes can be interpreted in several ways, depending on their appearance and placement on the paper. For example, a shape that resembles a heart may symbolize love, while a circle might represent unity or completeness. By interpreting the shapes you see, you can gain insight into your past, present, and future. Ink scrying is a simple but effective way to connect with your subconscious mind and uncover hidden truths.

Pros and Cons

Ink scrying is a relatively simple and inexpensive form of divination. All you need is a piece of paper, ink, coffee, or tea. Additionally, this method can be used for various purposes, from gaining self-knowledge to predicting the future. However, some drawbacks should be considered. One potential downside is that it can be difficult to interpret the shapes you see. If you're not experienced with this method, it's easy to mistake one shape for another.

Additionally, some people find that they become too focused on the patterns they see, which can prevent them from seeing the greater picture. If you find yourself getting too caught up in ink, it might be helpful to take a break and return to it later. Overall, ink scrying is a simple but powerful form of divination that can yield valuable insights. However, as with any type of divination, it's important to approach it with caution and an open mind.

Step-By-Step Instructions

If you're interested in trying ink scrying, all you need is a piece of paper, some ink, coffee, or tea. To get started, follow these simple steps:

1. Find a quiet place to work where you won't be disturbed.
2. Pour some ink, coffee, or tea onto a plate or shallow dish.
3. Dip your finger in the liquid and use it to draw shapes or patterns on a piece of paper.
4. As you look at the shapes you've created, allow your mind to wander and see what images or messages come to you.
5. Write down any insights you receive in a journal for future reference.

Smoke Scrying

Smoke scrying is a type of divination that involves observing the patterns formed by smoke. It can be done with any type of smoke, but incense is most commonly used. You may see images, symbols, or messages in the smoke. Allow whatever comes to you to be without judgment or analysis. Smoke scrying is a simple yet powerful way to connect with your intuition and receive guidance from the spirit world.

Pros and Cons

Many cultures have their methods of smoke scrying, and the practice has been used for centuries to help people make important decisions. There are pros and cons to smoke scrying, and it's crucial to weigh them before deciding whether this form of divination is right for you.

One of the biggest advantages of smoke scrying is that it can be done almost anywhere. All you need is a fire and some form of smoking material (such as herbs). This makes it a very convenient form of divination for people always on the go. Additionally, it can be a very personal experience. Since you interpret the smoke yourself, there is no need to rely on anyone else's opinion or interpretation. However, there are also some disadvantages.

One downside is that it can be difficult to correctly interpret the smoke. This form of divination requires a lot of practice and experience to become accurate. Additionally, because interpreting the smoke is such a personal experience, it's easy to let your biases influence your readings. Overall, smoke scrying is a unique and interesting form of divination with both pros and cons. Keep these in mind before deciding whether or not it's right for you.

Step-By-Step Instructions

If you're interested in trying smoke scrying, all you need is a fire and some form of smoking material (such as incense or herbs). To get started, follow these simple steps:

1. Find a quiet place to work where you won't be disturbed.
2. Light a fire in a safe place.
3. Add your smoking material to the fire.
4. Observe the patterns formed by the smoke.
5. Allow your mind to wander and see what images or messages come to you.
6. Write down any insights that you receive in a journal for future reference.

Overall, scrying is a powerful tool that can be used for divination and self-discovery. There are many different methods, each with its advantages and disadvantages. This chapter provides a brief overview of some of the most popular ones. Experiment with different techniques and find the one that works best for you. Remember to approach scrying with an open mind and let the information that comes to you flow in without judgment or analysis. With practice, you'll be able to use scrying to gain valuable insights into yourself and your life.

Chapter 10: Advanced Spirit World Communication Methods

Communicating with the spirit world can be a very rewarding experience. It can provide you with closure, answers to burning questions, or simply give you a sense of connection to something greater than yourself. In this chapter, we will explore some of the more advanced methods of spirit-world communication. These methods include using a pendulum, an Ouija board, tarot cards, and automatic writing. By the end of this chapter, you should understand how to use each of these methods and the pros and cons associated with each one.

Communicating with the spirit world can provide you with closure, answers to burning questions, or simply give you a sense of connection to something greater than yourself.
https://www.pexels.com/photo/hands-holding-the-crystal-ball-on-the-wooden-table-6806746/

Using a Pendulum for Spirit Communication

A pendulum is a weight, typically made of crystal, hung from a string or chain. Using one for spirit communication is a practice that dates back centuries. The pendulum is thought to be able to tap into the subconscious mind and connect with the spiritual realm. Pendulums are often used for divination and psychic readings. Many people believe that a pendulum can be used to communicate with the dead.

1. How to Use a Pendulum

There are a few different ways to use a pendulum for spirit communication. One way is to ask yes or no questions. The pendulum will swing in a certain direction to indicate the answer. Another way is to hold the pendulum over a sheet of paper with different symbols or words. The pendulum will swing toward the symbol or the word it is connected to.

If you are new to using a pendulum, it is best to start with simple questions. You may also want to have someone else hold the pendulum while you ask the questions. This will help eliminate any bias on your part. Once you get comfortable with using the pendulum, you can experiment with more complex questions. Remember, there are no wrong answers when communing with the spirits. Enjoy the process and see what wisdom they have to share with you!

2. Pros and Cons of Using a Pendulum

There are both pros and cons to using a pendulum for spirit communication. One pro is that it can be used by anyone, regardless of experience level. Another is that it does not require any special equipment or tools. All you need is a pendulum and something to write with. Pendulum use is not without its detractors. Some people believe that the pendulum can be influenced by the user's thoughts and feelings, making it unreliable as a method of communication. Others believe that the pendulum can be used to communicate with non-human entities, like demons and other dark forces. Despite these concerns, many people find the pendulum to be a useful tool for spirit communication and continue to use it.

3. Tips for Using a Pendulum

If you decide to use a pendulum for spirit communication, you should keep a few things in mind.

- Be in a relaxed state of mind. This will help you clear your mind and allow the pendulum to swing freely.

- Hold the pendulum over your dominant hand. This hand should be resting palm up on a flat surface.

- Ask your question out loud. This will help focus your thoughts and allow the pendulum to find the answer more easily.

- Be patient. The pendulum may not swing immediately. Give it a few moments to find the answer.

- Be open to whatever answer the pendulum gives. Remember, there are no wrong answers when communing with the dead.

Using a Ouija Board for Spirit Communication

A Ouija board is a board that is marked with the letters of the alphabet, numbers 0-9, and the words "yes," "no," and "hello." The board is used in conjunction with a planchette, a small heart-shaped piece of wood or plastic used to point to the different letters and symbols on the board. Many people believe that the Ouija board can be used to communicate with the dead.

1. How to Use a Ouija Board

Using a Ouija board is relatively simple. First, you need to gather a group of people together. Two is the minimum, but more can be used if desired. Next, you'll need to sit around the board and place your fingers on the planchette. Once everyone is ready, one person will ask a question out loud. The planchette will then begin to move around the board, spelling out the answer to the question.

2. Pros and Cons of Using a Ouija Board

Like any method of spirit communication, there are both pros and cons to using a Ouija board. One pro is that it can be a fun activity to do with friends or family. It can also connect with loved ones who have passed on. Another pro is that it is relatively easy to use and does not require special skills or knowledge.

There are also some cons. One is that it can be dangerous if not used correctly. There have been reports of people becoming possessed after using a Ouija board, so it is crucial to use caution. Another con is that the answers you receive may not always be accurate. This is because the planchette can be influenced by outside forces, such as wind or drafts.

3. Tips for Using a Ouija Board

If you decide to use a Ouija board, you should keep a few things in mind.

- Be respectful of the dead. This means not asking questions that could upset them or cause them to want to harm you.

- Be aware of your surroundings. Make sure that no drafts or wind could potentially move the planchette.

- Do not use the board alone. Always have at least one other person with you.

- Do not take the answers you receive at face value. Remember that they may not be accurate.

Using Tarot Cards for Spirit Communication

Tarot cards are cards used for divination. The deck is made up of 78 cards, which are divided into two groups: the Major Arcana and the Minor Arcana. The Major Arcana consists of 22 cards representing major life events or transitions. The Minor Arcana consists of 56 cards representing day-to-day challenges and experiences.

1. How to Use Tarot Cards for Spirit Communication

Tarot cards have been used for centuries as a tool for divination, but they can also be used for spirit communication. To use tarot cards for spirit communication, start by meditating and then asking your question out loud. Then, shuffle the deck and lay out the cards in a spread. Once the cards are laid out, focus on each one individually and ask your question again. As you do this, pay attention to any thoughts, feelings, or images that come to mind. These may be messages from your spirit guide or other spirits. If you're unsure what a message means, try looking up the card's symbolism in a book or online. With a little practice, you'll be able to use tarot cards for spirit communication.

2. Pros and Cons of Using Tarot Cards

Many people believe that tarot cards can be used as a tool for spirit communication. There are several different ways to use the cards for this purpose. While some people find tarot card readings to be accurate and helpful, others are skeptical of their ability to connect with spirits. Here are some pros and cons of using tarot cards for spirit communication:

Pros:

- Tarot card readings can be very accurate. Experienced readers can often interpret the messages of the cards very clearly.

- Readings can provide guidance and insight into important decisions. By connecting with spirits, tarot readers can receive guidance that may not be available through other means.

- These readings can be fun. Even if you don't believe in their ability to connect with spirits, tarot readings can be an enjoyable way to pass the time.

Cons:

- Some people believe that tarot card readings are inaccurate and misleading. There is no guarantee that the messages you receive from a tarot reading will be accurate or helpful.

- They can be expensive. If you hire a professional reader, you may have to pay quite a bit of money for their services.

- The readings can be intimidating. If you are unfamiliar with the process, it can be hard to know what to expect going into one.

3. Tips for Using Tarot Cards

If you decide to use tarot cards for spirit communication, you should keep a few things in mind.

- Make sure you are working with a reputable reader. There are many charlatans out there who will try to take advantage of people.

- Be clear about what you want to achieve from the reading. Before you begin, take some time to think about what you hope to gain from the experience. This will help you focus your questions and get the most out of the reading.

- Be open to the messages you receive. Don't try to force a particular outcome from the reading. Instead, let the messages come to you and trust that they are guidance from your spirit guide or other spirits.

Automatic Writing

Automatic writing is a spiritual practice that can be used to communicate with the other side. It is a form of channeling in which the writer surrenders their hand to a higher power and allows that higher power to write *through them*. This process can be done with a pen and paper or even with your finger if you are using a tablet or smartphone. The vital thing is to clear your mind and allow the words to flow. There is no need to worry about spelling or grammar, as the message will come through regardless. You may find that the words come slowly at first, but with practice, you'll be able to receive clear messages from your guides and loved ones who have passed on.

1. How to Perform Automatic Writing

Automatic writing is a simple process that anyone can do. It can be a powerful way to receive messages from the other side. To begin, find a quiet place where you will not be interrupted. Sit down with a pen and paper, and relax your mind. Once you feel calm, allow your hand to move freely across the page. As you write, trust that the words you receive are from the spirit world. The messages may not make sense at first, but if you keep writing, they will begin to form cohesive thoughts. If you keep an open mind, automatic writing can be a powerful tool for spirit communication.

2. Pros and Cons of Automatic Writing

There are many benefits to Automatic Writing. For one, it is a great way to receive messages from deceased loved ones. It can also be used to communicate with guides and angels. If you are looking for guidance on a particular issue, automatic writing can help you receive clarity.

There are also some drawbacks to Automatic Writing. It can be quite upsetting if you are not mentally or emotionally prepared to receive messages from the other side. Also, if you are not used to channeling energy, it can be easy to become fatigued. Setting aside time for relaxation before and after your session is crucial. Overall, this is a powerful tool that can be used for good or ill, depending on the user's intention. Use it wisely, and it will serve you well.

3. Tips for Automatic Writing

Here are a few tips to help you get the most out of your automatic writing experiences:

- Relax and clear your mind before beginning. The more relaxed you are, the easier it will be to receive messages.
- Set an intention for your session. What do you hope to achieve? Keep this in mind as you write.

- Be patient. The messages may not come immediately, but if you keep writing, they will come through.

- Be open to whatever comes through. You may not always understand the message, but trust that it is coming from a higher power.

- Take breaks as needed. If you feel tired or frustrated, take a break and return later.

- Keep a journal of your experiences. This will be a valuable resource to look back on later.

These are just a few of the many ways you can communicate with the other side. Experiment and find the method that works best for you. Always approach these experiences with an open mind and heart – and trust that the messages you receive are for your highest good. This chapter has provided some tips and background information on various mediumship methods. From here on, it is up to you to explore and find the ones that work best for you. So go forth and communicate with the other side!

Conclusion

Now that you have read all the information on mediumship, it's time to put it all together and start practicing! Remember, the most crucial thing is to relax and open yourself up to the experience. You'll be amazed at what you can do with a little practice!

This easy-to-follow guide has given you all the tools you need to develop your mediumship skills. It started with an introduction to the basics of mediumship and its workings. You learned about the different types of mediumship, as well as the astral body and the spirit world. You also learned some important techniques for grounding and preparing yourself before readings, as well as how to recognize energy.

After that, you dove right in, learning how to develop your clairvoyance skill. You also discovered spirit channeling and how to channel your spirit guides. Finally, you learned about advanced spirit world communication methods, like scrying, cleansing, and protecting yourself. The key to success is to relax and have fun with it!

If you want to try channeling your guides, start by doing some basic research. You can find plenty of resources online or at your local library. Once you understand the basics well, find a quiet place to relax and focus your thoughts. You may want to light a candle or burn some incense to help you relax and to create a sacred space. Then, simply ask your guides to come forward and communicate with you. You may want to ask specific questions or simply allow them to speak through you. Trust your intuition and go with whatever feels right.

Scrying is another great way to communicate with the spirit world. You can use a crystal ball, a bowl of water, a mirror, or any other shiny surface. Simply gaze into the surface and allow your mind to relax. You may see images or receive messages from your guides. Don't worry if you don't see or hear anything right away. It takes practice to develop your mediumistic abilities. Just keep trying, and eventually, you'll be amazed at what you can do.

While mediumship is a great way to connect with the spirit world, protecting yourself from negative energy is crucial. There are a few simple things you can do to protect yourself. First, always cleanse yourself and your space before you begin a session. You can use sage, salt water, or any other method you feel comfortable with. Second, always set your intention before you begin. Make sure that you are only working with positive, benevolent spirits. Finally, trust your intuition. If something doesn't feel right, just stop and walk away.

Mediumship is a great way to connect with the spirit world and receive guidance from your loved ones. You'll be amazed at what you can do with a little practice! Just remember to relax, go with your intuition, and have fun with it.

Here's another book by Mari Silva that you might like

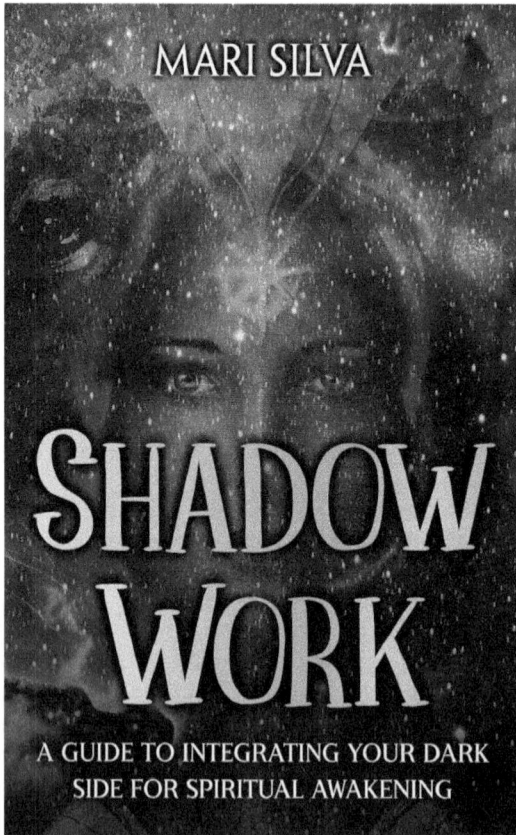

MARI SILVA

SHADOW WORK

A GUIDE TO INTEGRATING YOUR DARK
SIDE FOR SPIRITUAL AWAKENING

Your Free Gift
(only available for a limited time)

Thanks for getting this book! If you want to learn more about various spirituality topics, then join Mari Silva's community and get a free guided meditation MP3 for awakening your third eye. This guided meditation mp3 is designed to open and strengthen ones third eye so you can experience a higher state of consciousness. Simply visit the link below the image to get started.

https://spiritualityspot.com/meditation

References

Aletheia. (2016, March 10). Scrying: How to practice the ancient art of second sight (with pictures). LonerWolf. https://lonerwolf.com/scrying/

Board of Directors. (2013, April 11). What is a medium? Eomega.org; Omega Institute. https://www.eomega.org/article/what-is-a-medium

Psychic mediums. (n.d.). Osu.edu. https://u.osu.edu/vanzandt/2018/03/08/psychic-mediums-2/

Smith, G. (2017). Mediumship: An introductory guide to developing spiritual awareness and intuition. Hay House UK.

Spiritualism and mediumship. (2019, August 29). Understanding Voices; Hearing the Voice. https://understandingvoices.com/exploring-voices/voices-and-spirituality/case-studies/spiritualism-and-mediumship/

Wahbeh, H., & Radin, D. (2018). People reporting experiences of mediumship have higher dissociation symptom scores than non-mediums but below thresholds for pathological dissociation. F1000Research, 6, 1416. https://doi.org/10.12688/f1000research.12019.3

Wigington, P. (2013, October 12). What Does Scrying Mean? Learn Religions. https://www.learnreligions.com/what-is-scrying-2561865